STRESS OUT

STRESS OUT

Show stress who's the boss!

Sumner M. Davenport

And introducing co-authors
and other contributors

Self Investment Publishing

Self-Investment Publishing

2219 E. Thousand Oaks Blvd. #102-386

Thousand Oaks, Ca 91362

Graphics Jana Plommer, Jackson Gardner, Steven Meyers

Research & Editing, Sumner M. Davenport © 2009

Published by Self-Investment Publishing © 2009

10 9 8 7 6 5 1 4 3 2 1

ISBN 10: 0-9815238-3-8
ISBN 13: 978-0-9815238-3-5

Introducing co-authors and other contributors

Aila Accad, RN, MSN
Support with Coaching and Counseling
Job Stress

Debra Costanzo
8 Really, Really Good Reasons to Hire a Virtual Assistant
Take Heed, Take a Break

Gina Cotroneo
How to Land Sunny Side Up

Jerilynn Draker
Zzzzzzzz

Beverly Edelstein
Just Scream

Monika Klein, BS, CN
What Are You Eating and What's Eating You?

Nancy Miiller
Honor Yourself
Forgiveness

Veronica Ray
Change the Channel

Ellen Whitehurst
Take a Bath Tip
Foot Reflexology Tip

Melissa Whuel
Change Location

Testimonials and other contributors:

Marcia Bearn
Julie Cucina
Tracy Gelfer
Michelle Granger
Cameron Grover
Precilla Junart
Barbara Kramer
Lisa Lorie
Tracy Marine
Pat Mynor
Cathi Polenetic
Brad Smorther
Marcie Taylor

Dedication

This book is dedicated to Lancelot,
who taught me unconditional love.

Table of Contents

Although every chapter offers solutions, and many provide quick action steps you can take, we have highlighted a few Quick tips on the next page. You can also find these quick tips in the book next to the QT

$\mathcal{QT}$ Quick Tips

INTRODUCTION

"If you ask what is the single most important key to longevity,
I would have to say it is avoiding worry, stress and tension.
And if you didn't ask me, I'd still have to say it."
~ George F. Burns ~

My research for this book was motivated because like so many other people, I was overwhelmed by the stress in my life. I was feeling that my resources and solutions were limited and ineffective. Because of intense stressful events in my life my normal resilience was weakened. It was difficult to manage routine tasks effectively, it was difficult to relax, my sleeping was restless, my emotions were always right on the surface, my energy was low, excessive noise in public places was intolerable and I felt helpless. Over the years I had learned different coping techniques but now they either weren't working for me or I needed new input on how to do them more efficiently.

At times when I reached out for help, I often heard to "just think positive". Thinking positive is difficult to do when your world seems to be falling apart and you feel alone. When the problems appear to loom larger than the solutions, hope for a solution can be the faintest glimmer in the far distance; and without hope, positive thinking is impossible. When I talked to other people who were dealing with several stressful life issues and events at the same time, the effect of all of these events outweighed their perceived abilities to find something positive to think about. And when they could, it seemed like a nano-second of thought and that seemed more futile than helpful.

Standing in lines at the places where I shopped and conducted business, the topic of stress seemed to be part of many of the reactions to minor occurrences which then invoked various conversations. I began to ask these people about their stress solutions and stress release techniques. Everyone had something they used, mostly occasionally, and yet they were still looking for something more effective or easier. Through the polls and surveys I placed on the internet asking the same questions, I received dozens of responses, some offering techniques and solutions and others asking for help. This book is a collection from many of those communications, including testimonials and shared stories.

There are also many qualified coaches, therapists and workshops leaders teaching stress response solutions and life enhancing programs. As this book neared it's preparation to be printed, I wanted it to offer even more than just the results of my interviews so I invited some of these experts in their fields to participate and write a chapter or more.

This gives you, the reader, solutions that you may not have otherwise considered, or be reminded of something you already knew and temporarily forgot; plus meet coaches who can help you if you need additional support. And for these co-authors, this book is the opportunity to get their message and expertise in front of more people who they can potentially now help with their stress.

This book offers you a selection of resources in the form of advice from experts, suggestions from the experiences of others, some in quick tips and others in more detail. You might enjoy reading the book from cover to cover and selecting your favorites or you might use the book for a quick answer by letting it drop open to any place in the book and reading and following that suggestion. The intention of Stress Out is to provide you several options to help you find the ones that work for you.

Some people will read this book and respond only to the logical step-by-step instructions; whereas other people will engage themselves into the stories. Depending on what your stress level is at the time you pick up this book, you will find a reading style that helps you find your answers.

The focus of this book is **STRESS OUT**, not Stressed Out. Stressed-out is a condition you may be experiencing; Stress Out is a solution, a command to tell stress who's the boss. This book includes detailed, duplicatable tips, tools and techniques that you can use to reduce, release and/or manage your stressful reactions.

This book does not contain all the answers or available techniques and tools I heard and discovered. These suggestions may not help pay your rent, fix your broken car, get your job back or take away those pesky 20 extra pounds; however, they may help you to feel better so you can face whatever shows up in your life with more peace and confidence.

PLUS a website has been created to support you with additional articles, links and resources. The website will be referenced in strategic places throughout this book to identify products, services, and free downloads mentioned in specific chapters. A Stress Out Daily Tips opt-in e-zine will provide a daily tip, as well as special offers we find that can support you in showing stress who's the boss. The website address and e-zine information are located in the Resource Section at the back of this book.

Books are still considered one of our comfort items. Curl up with a good book and a cup of tea or hot cocoa and you can lose yourself in the pages. The intention of this book is to be a solution to your search by bringing together several suggestions, expert tips and personal stories from people who are successfully using these techniques. I have practiced several of the suggestions made in this book. Some worked better for me than others. When you choose a tool or technique that you have never tried before, or one that you haven't used for a long time, give yourself a chance to adapt to it. Old habits are going to surface, even as you work to establish new ones. Repetition over a few days or a few times will give you a better assessment if your new choice is working for you.

Publishers note: This book is designed to provide suggestions in the form of comments, testimonials, personal stories, and advice and action steps. It is not intended as medical or psychological advice. The results a person may receive from following the suggestions in this book are subjective and unique to each individual. There is no guarantee implied or otherwise, that following any of these recommendations will correct the causes of your stress or definitely eliminate the distress you are feeling. The responsibility for use and practice and the results obtained are solely the responsibility of the readers of this book.

WHO ME? STRESSED?!

Are you *STRESSED* !?

Stress is a constant in our lives - such a constant that we actually don't realize we are under stress, we think it's "just part of life." Health surveys report that over 70% of people feel stress everyday.

We experience traffic jams, deadlines, eating on the run, we stress when we have bills to pay, job changes, endless chores and too many errands. Our job has stress, not having a job has stress, it's stressful maintaining your weight, having a relationship is stressful, not being in a relationship is stressful, family responsibilities are stress, and all those other demands on you can be huge amounts of stress. Not to mention those people who really get on your nerves.

There is something stressing someone everyday and everywhere! You are not alone. But is there anything that can be done?

There are so many recommendations for reducing stress, but what really works?

Something you do everyday may be different than something you need to do when the stress meter rises.

Most people will tell you that they want stress out of their lives. Hearing that stress is a normal part of human existence and stress is everywhere, these same people will tell you that they at least want stress out of the driver's seat in their life. They want better control of their responses and the effects stress is having on them. Stress and anxiety is estimated to affect well over 19 million Americans and growing. One factor contributing to increasing levels of substance abuse is related to this person's perception of their level of stress and their ability to do something about it.

You may have searched the internet for answers and found one suggestion at one website you visited that made sense to you, and you searched longer and found another one on another site and with more research you may have found more. And the more time you spent on the internet looking for solutions, the more stress you began to feel. You may have found, like I did, information that talked more about the problem and less about solutions.

Searching for and finding a tool or technique is only one part of the equation in your stress solution. Showing stress who's the boss starts with your willingness to change. To this point you have been using certain reactions and behaviors to deal with your stress. You are here because you need more or a new perspective. For any of the information in this book to work for you, you must be willing to read and then apply the suggestions with an open mind. You must be willing to take action and commit to doing your selected stress solution more than once to see a measureable result in your life, and in some cases, your body. Our life changes when we change our behaviors.

> *"The definition of Insanity is doing the same things and expecting different results."*
> ~ Albert Einstein ~

Just about everyone knows that stress is in part of their lives. It is hard to read a newspaper or watch a television program without hearing about stress. We continue to hear and read that stress may contribute to the development of some illnesses, including heart disease and cancer. Although is seems that everyone talks about stress, according to a recent studies, only 28% of people claim to be in control over their stress. However over 75% of those interviewed also complained about physical symptoms related to stress.

"It's not stress that kills us; it is our reaction to it."
~ Hans Selye ~

Stress is not new, Years ago psychologists reported that stress can be thought of as resulting from an "imbalance between demands and resources" or as occurring when "pressure exceeds one's perceived ability to cope".

No two people are affected in exactly the same way, or to the same degree, but most people living in our highly industrialized society suffer from effects of stress at one or more times during their lives. There is a range of physical symptoms related to stress, ranging from minor headaches to severe physical ailments. At one time it was believed that is was only a selected list of life events that could bring on stress. As our technology has evolved, our communities and family dynamics have changed; the length of list has expanded. Over 50% of people believe that we have more stress today than our parents, and certainly their parents did. Thousands of people visit their doctors every year with physical ailments related to stress and you may be one of them!

The effects of stress, even if due to the same event or situation, can cause different reactions and illnesses in each person. Your existing health and physical condition can also add to the difference in your responses when facing something that causes you to feel stressed. One person may feel invigorated with starting a new business or changing jobs, and someone else will feel stressed with all the responsibilities. That also explains why some stress release tools and techniques work differently for each person.

Because of the overabundance of stress in our daily modern lives, we usually think of stress only as a negative experience, but stress can be a neutral, negative, and sometimes even a positive experience. A little of this stress can help keep you on your toes, ready to rise to a challenge. Too much stress can harm your attitude, your motivation and your health – it can age you and **it can kill you.**

You may have heard or read information about how stress harms your body and your health, and just hearing that information causes you even more stress and can make it difficult for you to find solutions that you can follow to do something about it. While we deal with high levels of stress on a daily basis, the health consequences are most serious when we attempt to manage our stress in unhealthy ways. Almost half of us overeat or eat foods that are unhealthy as an attempt to quiet or push down our feelings of stress. Almost 40% of people have a few (or more) drinks and admit to drinking to excess when they begin to feel too much stress. With all the negative press surrounding cigarettes, the number of smokers may have decreased, however of those that smoke, recent polls indicate that two-thirds report they smoke more when they feel out of control with their stress. However each of these cases, drinking and smoking are still their first choice, even though they admit it doesn't actually help.

> *"Stress will only increase with your permission.*
> *If you desire more of it, do nothing.*
> *If you desire less of it, do something.*
> *If you've been doing nothing,*
> *doing something means everything!"*
> ~ Debra Costanzo ~

While many people recognize the negative impact their stress has on their health and the other areas in their life, they seem overwhelmed at how to make behavior changes. The responses to my various polls and inquiries indicated that techniques with specific step by step instructions were more helpful than a bulleted laundry list. And too many choices had a tendency of feeling overwhelming, not being able to decide which one to try first.

The motivating factor that reportedly makes the difference does not come from "well meaning" or pushy family or friends. The motivation comes from within. The most significant changes were made when they were fed up with feeling bad, feeling loss of control over their lives and had an intense desire to just feel better. Many believed this could be accomplished if they could reduce their unconscious or negative reactions to stress. Motivation for their own personal reasons started them on the path to finding new resources and implementing effective behavior changes in their life. Studies show that a desire to improve their self image or self esteem was also a strong motivator. Encouragement from close relationships was more welcomed after their self motivated decision was already made.

There are many tools that can be learned and practiced that when followed consistently, give support to managing and surviving and even thriving from stress. The intensity of the stress may require more than one tool or technique. How a person practices stress management before it hits, has much to do with how they handle the stressor when it shows up. Some people have never learned a stress management tool that works for them, others use techniques sporadically. Most of the people I interviewed only a few claimed that they do anything on a regular or consistent basis to keep their stress in healthy levels.

Working on this book challenged my ability to handle stress. Coordinating co-authors, graphic artists, marketing, editing, deadlines as well as other responsibilities with my clients and my personal life, it was challenging and fun. Fortunately I had the pages of this book in front of me everyday as a handy and important resource. Keep this book handy, whether you read it cover to cover or just visit it from time to time by opening to any page, and you may find it easier and easier to show stress who's the boss.

Stress is your body's response which includes a combination of physical, mental, and emotional feelings resulting from feeling pressured, guilt from the past, and worry about events, people and circumstances – real or perceived. Stress is anxiety, frustration, a feeling of loss of control. Surprising as it may seem, some stress does have positive outcomes and can help you deal with the challenges of your life. If you are an athlete, good stress can give you the energy you need in a physical competition. Some people actually excel under deadlines because the stress helps them to establish positive boundaries, and within those boundaries their creativity is called upon.

Stress can be beneficial when it motivates you, inspires you, excites you when you are striving for a desired goal, encourages you to make positive changes in your life, but can

be deadly when it is the stress that your body reacts to with ill health and disease. When it's too much to handle, your body and emotional balance can break down. Too many people go to their doctors every year with unspecific symptoms of not feeling themselves.

So many times we treat our automobiles better than we treat our mental and physical bodies. That vehicle we travel in everywhere is out physical body and it needs great care to continue to function properly. You probably wouldn't think of jump starting your car in the morning, cold start without fuel and then running it nonstop at full throttle all day. It's unlikely that you would never shut off the engine and instead run your car engine at its optimum, in high gear, constantly revving the engine for more power, driving it continually and with no service break or down time. If you were to treat your car this way, you know that it would start to break down, usually at the most inconvenient times. It would become less reliable, and cause you more stress.

Yet, many people jump start their days still overheated from the day before; run themselves in high gear, overheated, under fed and with poor fuel, over accelerated with a constant push and no breaks. Then we wonder why we are feeling so poorly and less effective?!

Unhealthy stress can take an emotional as well as physical toll, in the form of anxiety, depression, high blood pressure, heart disease and several other serious illnesses. If unattended stress can seriously your damage physical health, your psychological well-being; and your relationships with your friends, family, and co-workers. There is no better time than now to get serious and start decreasing the effects of stress in your life.

There are dozens of ways you can work with and through stress and maintain a healthy life regardless of the external events. These can include many popular techniques you have already heard of, some you have forgotten and new methods are being proven in people's lives every day. Old or new, the solutions included in the Stress Out book are the result of long personal research. Each chapter is based on everyday insights, techniques and tools used by everyday people - like you.

START NOW

In many of my research conversations I heard statements such as "I'll start thinking of things to do to deal with stress after "this event", "this task", "this situation" (fill in the blank) is over. Once I get through, or finish (whatever it is) I'll stop smoking, or start exercising, or change my diet.

Although there are some things you can put off until tomorrow, the sooner you take steps to assist you with your stress, the sooner you will see the results.

► So before taking that next cigarette - take a breath.

► Before reaching for that alcoholic drink - drink a glass of water instead.

► Before walking to the refrigerator to get something. sweet - be sweet to yourself and walk around the room, and if you have time, around the block.

► Turn the page and start reading ways to show stress who's the boss.

► And above all - Breathe!

MEDICAL ADVICE

The recommendations in this book are not intended as a source of medical or psychological advice. Nor should they be considered a replacement for the advice and recommendations your medical doctor or medical practitioner have given you. If you are having a physical or psychiatric emergency, please call 911 or go to your nearest emergency room or urgent care facility.

 There are several ways to treat the effects of stress on your body and emotions. Some of these solutions include prescriptive medicine. Many conventional doctors are also recognizing the benefits of complimentary medicine in treating not only the effects but the cause of the stress damage.

If you are already feeling the effects of stress in your body and your life, getting a thorough medical exam and opinion is an important step. Assessing any damage already starting or present in your body can be helpful when determining which solutions are best for you.

Your health professional can help you to understand your symptoms and the causes, if stress related or otherwise. There are several conventional and complimentary medical solutions to assist you in dealing with stress in your life. I strongly recommend you work in partnership with your medical practitioner on your health. Many medical doctors today are recommending alternative practices to their patients, some in support of and others in place of medications. These can include, massage, acupuncture, counseling, chiropractic, yoga, exercise therapy, etc. A few complimentary practices are referred to in various chapters throughout this book.

If you are taking a doctor prescribed medication it is important to continue as prescribed. Equally important, it is dangerous to self diagnose to self prescribe medical drugs. Because of tough financial times, and lack of health insurance, many people are not visiting their doctors regularly and are resorting to self diagnosis with the help of the internet. The easy availability of medications on the internet has prompted people to buy and dispense their own medications at their own diagnosis. Although the internet is filled with information, some of it is actually false and misleading. Other medical information can be confusing to a person not educated in the language. Potential problems with self prescribing through the internet can range from receiving improper medications which do nothing to help, to addiction and overdose. Some drugs can become addictive when used in excess of their intended use, and other drugs may conflict with other medications you may also be taking. Many drugs have side effects and without the assistance of your medical doctor and/or pharmacist you may actually be causing your self more harm than good.

Generally speaking, complimentary methods focus on preventing disease and work by assisting your body to heal itself. A person can contribute to his own healing when you pay personal attention to your body's reactions and healing. The same method of complimentary medical treatment cannot be suitable for everyone since each person's body, emotional acceptance is unique. This is why two people diagnosed with the same stress symptoms, not only react differently, they heal differently.

It can be very stressful not have health insurance. Some people without health insurance find this to be a wake up call to put more effort into healthy self care to get and stay healthy. It can be stressful to worry about your health, so taking care of your health in positive ways can help alleviate some of your stress related to worry.

It is important to pay attention to your health and find simple solutions to treat your minor ailments rather than running to the doctor for every little thing. It is empowering to take responsibility for your health, and find healthy solutions you can live with.

Check your television shows. Many local news stations and talk shows are adding health segments. National shows like Dr. Oz, PBS and the Discovery Channel deliver televised segments dedicated to health, and post follow-up and additional information on their websites. WebTV shows are showing up on the internet at an increasing rate, by both medical professionals and stress coaches.

There are a few places you can still receive medical care without insurance and for reduced and sometimes no cost.

1. Under the Hill Burton Law, you might qualify for free health care at specific health facilities. To find out if you or someone you know qualifies and what you need to know, visit their website at
   http://www.hrsa.gov/hillburton/hillburtonfacilities.htm

2. Ask your doctor if they allow a discount for cash payments. Your doctor is interested in your well being. Some doctors appreciate not having to file the paperwork and hassle with an insurance company for their payment.

3. Watch for health fairs and mobile health screenings. Sometimes having a few tests run, and hearing healthy results can give you peace of mind. I recently had a series of tests run by a mobile health testing unit. Getting the printout of positive results that indicated I had no serious health concerns was just what I needed. These testing services usually screen to detect carotid artery stenosis, arterial fibrillation, abdominal aortic aneurysms, peripheral arterial disease, bone density, finger stick blood screenings for lipid panel, glucose and

a few other tests. These screening services make people aware of an undetected health problem, and these services encourage you to seek follow up care with your physician. It can be a place to start.

4. Check with your local county hospital or teaching hospital. Some offer discounts programs for people without medical insurance.

5. Locate a Free Clinic in your area. Free clinics provide a range of medical, dental, pharmacy, and/or behavioral health services to economically disadvantaged individuals who are predominately uninsured. Some free clinics actually charge a nominal fee to their patients; however they still deliver essential services regardless of the patient's ability to pay. To locate a Free Clinic in your area visit: http://freeclinics.us

CHECKING YOUR STRESS LEVEL

If you've been wondering what degree of stress you live under, there are a few quick ways to get a fair estimate.

1. **Keep a stress journal for** one week.

In this journal make a note of which events and situations caused you to feel a response that you would label as stress. These responses include physical, emotional and mental responses. Each event and each response may be different.

With each entry take a moment to observe what you are actually feeling and thinking. Record the time and describe what happened. Where were you; what happened; what triggered it (someone or something); and who else was involved. Describe what you were feeling in your body, and what emotions did you feel, and express. Also, describe your reaction. Did you say something or do something?

Finally, on a scale of 1 (not very intense) to 10 (very intense), rate the intensity of your stress related to this event or circumstance. And very important, how long did it take you to get over this, if you did?

STRESS JOURNAL	
Date Time	Intensity 1-10 ☐
WHERE	
WHAT happened	
TRIGGERED by	
WHO else was involved	
My **PHYSICAL** **FEELINGS**	
My **EMOTIONAL** **FEELINGS**	
My **REACTIONS**	
My **RECOVERY**	

A stress journal sheet is available as a free download at
www.stressout-book.com/stress-resources.htm

By reviewing your journal, you may begin to recognize your personal patterns in what stresses you and how you react. If you used a stress release technique or management tool and doing so led you to a quicker recovery, this action may be your best response to this type of stressor.

On the other hand if you felt out of control, physically or emotionally bothered for a long time afterwards, you may want to consider different ways to train and prepare yourself to respond to stress.

2.   For some people it is helpful to see a printed or visual assessment of their stress level from a medical professional. Over 20 years ago, Drs. Thomas and Richard Rahe began studying stress and from their

findings composed a table of events and the amount of stress each cause. The most interesting feature of this table is that the people they interviewed actually told them that they determined they could rate specific events for the stress they cause. So this stress assessment tool is human rather than a medical appraisal. The Doctors determined that the higher your stress reaction to certain events (stressors) the greater your risk of developing stress related illnesses unless you take healthy measures to respond to the stress. The more stressed you are to any one particular stressor; the more important you should work to find a positive solution to eliminate or at least change that stressor.

3. StressLess Company offers a free online assessment of your stress. Their online questionnaire is designed to help you quickly evaluate five important aspects of your stress. The 211 questions cover: *Work/Personal Life Stressors, Close Relationships, Health Conditions, Your Signs and Symptoms of Stress and The Effectiveness of your current Coping skills.* After you receive your results, you then have an option to request a custom designed program based on your results.

You can find links to these stress tests, plus a free download of the stress journal at:
www.stressout-book.com/stress-resources.htm

BREATHING IS ESSENTIAL

"Breath is the bridge which connects life to consciousness"
~ Thich Nhat Hahn ~

Your breath says more about you than what you may have eaten for lunch. Breathing is your body's way of getting oxygen into your blood and expelling the waste CO_2 gas.

Your body can survive without food for weeks, without water for days; but unless you are David Blaine, who broke the Guinness world record on the Oprah show by holding his breath for over 17 minutes, you can only go a few minutes without breathing before health problems begin to occur in your body.

Breathing is really kinda important ☺ and your breath can be an indicator of your emotional state of stress as well as a tool to show stress that you have control.

For most people, our breathing changes when we are stressed and we will begin to breath shallow and rapidly, whether we are thinking about it or physically participating in something that is causing us to feel stressed.

Just as you unconsciously learned to breathe shallow under stress, you can consciously train your breathing so that you will breathe fully at any time. This may seem silly to some people since breathing is an automatic function. However, stress breathing can become a habit. Although most of us breathe automatically without the aid of machines, we can still alter our breathing habits and patterns, either to support or to cause harm to our health.

Shallow stress breathing can lead to a decrease range of motion of your chest wall and eventually making it more difficult for you to actually be capable of taking in deep breaths without extra effort. When you breathe shallow or rapidly when you are stressed, your chest does not expand as much as it would with slower fuller breaths. Plus since you are using primarily only the top of your lung tissue, it is forced to do all the work. The primary role of your lungs is to get oxygen to your blood. The more you breathe shallow, the less oxygen is transferred to your blood, which then makes it difficult for your blood to do its job of transferring nutrients to your tissues.

Most people who are "chest" breathing are not aware that they are doing this. When you chest breath, your shoulders may rise with your inhale and your chest may expand. When you breathe fully, your abdomen expands with your breathing as well.

Here is an easy method that you can use right now, to see for yourself if you are a chest breather. Rest one of your hands on your chest and your other hand on your abdomen. Take in and exhale a few breaths and observe which hand moves or rises the most. If your hand on your chest rises more, you are a chest breather. If your hand which is on your abdomen moves more, you are an abdomen breather.

Some people learn the habit of chest breathing also when they hold their stomach in to attempt to create an illusion of being thinner or to try to fit into or wear tight clothes. On the other hand, people with extended stomachs or loose clothing don't necessarily breathe fully with their abdomens.

When you are breathing into your abdomen, you are working with your diaphragm. There are benefits of abdominal breathing. Singers, athletes and actors are trained to focus on their diaphragm when breathing to improve their stamina both physically and in performing. Public speakers are taught to breathe with the support of their diaphragm to boost their feelings of self confidence and voice projection. Breathing fully with the support of your diaphragm improves the flow of blood back to your heart and fills your lung's air pockets which help your lungs to remain healthy.

You can re-learn to breathe fully. Once you re-learn how to breathe and observe how good you feel from breathing fully, you will find it easier to keep your breathing full and relaxed anytime you begin to feel the effects of stress. With regular practice you will again breathe fully the majority of the time, even without having to consciously think about it.

Your diaphragm is a large muscle between the cavity of your chest and your abdomen, and it is the most important muscle you use when you breathe. When you inhale it causes your abdomen to expand; and combined with your chest muscles, your chest area also expands.

Breathing fully using the support of your diaphragm is an excellent relaxation tool that can reduce your stress and help you achieve an overall sense of well being.

QT

BREATHING EXERCISES:

To begin, observe your breathing right now.
❖ How are you breathing?
❖ Are you breathing shallow or deep?
❖ Are you breathing high so only your chest and maybe your shoulders rise; or do you feel your tummy expand and reduce with each breath?

Even though these are easy breathing exercises, if you have any feelings of discomfort – call your doctor. If you feel lightheaded when doing these, sit down. If you have any difficulty breathing – call your doctor. If you are currently under doctor care, check with your doctor about any exercise or deep breathing exercises.

STANDING BREATHING RELAX EXERCISE
1. Stand relaxed with both feet firmly on the ground or floor.
2. Place your feet comfortable apart, usually in line with your hips.
3. Take in a deep breath and reach up over your head, comfortably not stretching; bring you arms straight up, reaching to the sky (or roof in you are inside) with your elbows parallel to your ears.
4. Keeping your arms straight, exhale, and lower your arms until they are horizontal at your sides.
5. Take in a deep breath in this position, then slowly exhale, relaxing your shoulders and keeping your arms level.
6. Inhale and again reach up over your head, comfortably not stretching; bring you arms straight up, reaching up with your elbows parallel to your ears.
7. Exhale and lower your arms, relaxed at your sides.
8. Repeat this a few times and observe how differently you feel.

"For breath is life,
and if you breathe well you will live long on earth."
~Sanskrit Proverb ~

LAYING DOWN ABDOMINAL BREATHING EXERCISE
I learned this next breathing exercise from one of my meditation teachers. It is not only excellent at teaching you abdominal breathing, you can use this same breathing exercise to begin a meditation. This breathing exercise is offered to assist you to re-learn abdominal breathing. Practicing this at least twice a day will help you towards remembering to breathe fully, especially when you are experiencing stress.

1. Lay down on face up on a comfortable firm surface.
2. Place one hand on your chest and the other on your abdomen.
3. Start by exhaling fully through your mouth, and then inhaling through your nose. When you take a deep breath in, your hand on your abdomen should rise higher than the one on your chest.
4. Take a slow deep breath in through your nose; and then hold it while you count silently to 5 (or as long as you are able, not exceeding 8)
5. Slowly exhale through your mouth for a count of 8. Immediately after you exhale, gently contract your abdominal muscles to help you completely empty exhale your remaining breath. In general, your exhale should be twice as long as your inhale. Medical studies show that we deepen our breathing capabilities not by inhaling more air but more through exhaling it completely.
6. Repeat this five more times.

By laying your hands on your chest and your abdomen, they are intended to help you to see your breathing pattern and help you to re-learn how to breathe fully using the support of your diaphragm.

"Inhale, and God approaches you.
Hold the inhalation, and God remains with you.
Exhale, and you approach God.
Hold the exhalation, and surrender to God."
~Krishnamacharya ~

A few people have reported to me that when they first practiced abdominal breathing, they felt they wanted to cry. It is common for people to hold their breath as a method to hold back tears in certain situations, or when they don't want someone to see them cry. So if tears come up when you breathe fully and relaxed, they could be tears that have been held back for a long time or they could be tears of relief. You will know the difference. If emotions arise that you are feeling unprepared to handle, you may consider consulting with a coach or counselor.

"You know that our breathing is the inhaling and exhaling of air.
The organ that serves for this is the lungs that lie round the heart, so
that the air passing through them thereby envelops the heart. Thus
breathing is a natural way to the heart.
And so, having collected your mind within you, lead it into the
channel of breathing through which air reaches the heart and,
together with this inhaled air, force your mind to descend into the
heart and to remain there."
~ Nicephorus the Solitary ~

For another breathing exercise see the chapter Stretch, Breathe, Laugh.

ℚᴛ **BLOW BUBBLES**

Remember the carefree days when you were a kid playing? One of many children's favorite toys were bubbles.

There are several mentions of children blowing bubbles, in stories and paintings, using ruggedly made devices.

Prior to the 20th century, children discovered their mothers' leftover washing soap was fun to use to blow bubbles. In the early 1900's bubbles gained popularity when they were first packaged and sold as a toy

If you were a child of the 60's you might remember bubbles as a symbol of peace and harmony. The air was filled with bubbles as a symbol of peace and "flower power", instead of war. Bubbles were one representation of the flower children during that time.

Today, bubble solution is the best selling toy in the world! Millionaires have been made from various bubble blowing devices and solutions. One man has made a career as the world's largest bubble blower.

Blowing bubbles require you to breathe deeply and you create something beautiful in your exhale with the bubbles.

When I was a volunteer Guardian ad Litem with the Court Appointed Special Advocates (CASA) for the Los Angeles Superior court, I spent much of my time in the children's protective area with them as they waited anxiously for their individual time in the courtroom. Part of my responsibility was to assist them in knowing that they were not to blame and feeling as safe as possible when they faced the judge. Most of the children were scared and several kept quietly to themselves, and others were crying. One particular day I took a small bottle of bubbles with me and sitting with the child I was responsible for, we took turns blowing bubbles. In a matter of minutes we were surrounded by almost all of the other children and they wanted to blow bubbles too. We all shared in the bubble blowing fun and some of the tears were turned to laughter. Although the children still were fearful of the situation they were in, the moments they spent blowing bubbles and laughing relieved the stress in the room. Some of them actually walked to the courtroom with a smile on their face.

So keep a bottle of bubbles handy. Most toy stores still sell them for under a dollar. Surprise yourself, and maybe a few other people, by blowing a few bubbles the next time you feel stress. You might remember how fun this really is.

QT

If you don't have any bubbles handy, you can pretend and still see some positive results. Hold your thumb and first finger as if you were holding a bubble blower. Blow over the top of these two fingers as if the bubble blower circle was there at the top of your fingers. For extra emphasis, you can close your eyes and visualize the bubbles floating away and popping the air.

WHAT'S ON YOUR MIND?

*"The greatest weapon against stress
is our ability to choose one thought over another."*
~ William James ~

If you listened to your own words, and believe it or not, many people don't, are you affirming stress or are you affirming your strengths and abilities to find solutions to your stress?

Do you ever hear yourself say - "I am so stressed", "there is nothing I can do", "this is hopeless", "I can't to this (or that)"," this is a hopeless situation", "I'll never be able to handle or survive this", "I can't stand this", "this situation is killing me", "I knew it would turn out bad", "traffic is always bad", "(circumstance/person) is always like that", any statement that confirms *in advance* that the circumstances are going to be difficult, or any other similar statements?

Each one of these statements is depressing to think about, but to commit to it and rethink it over and over again, drains all hope and creative thinking that might have inspired you to a solution. That is a very helpless place to be; and who wouldn't be stressed with that!

How many times do you speak solutions? How many times do you say – "I can do this?", "this setback is only temporary", or anything similar to this?

The statements you affirm repeatedly, many times by habit, and can add to or help to relieve your stress and your stress reactions. When you made slight changes in your words, studies indicate that you can find a difference in your stress level, and your eventual results.

The word "affirmation" is usually referred to as a repeated positive statement; however an affirmation means is "to endorse or to express commitment to whatever is being said." A positive affirmation is a statement of a desired positive condition of your thoughts and circumstances, and a negative affirmation is committing to the negative perception or opinion.

Some people erroneously think that affirmations are a New Age game; yet psychologists, therapists and spiritual leaders have been counseling their clients for years to change their thoughts and words into positive statements and to repeat these statements often. In various religions we are told that our thoughts make us who we are, work for and against us, and make the world we live in.

"As a man thinketh in his heart, so is he."
~ Proverbs 23:7 ~

"We are what we think. All that we are arises with our thoughts. With our thoughts we make the world."
~ Dhammapada, Buddha ~

"Every thought we hold and every word we utter creates a positive or negative angel."
~ Kabbalah ~

Norman Vincent Peale, a protestant Minister authored the book, "The Power of Positive Thinking" in 1953 and he has been acknowledged as a progenitor of the theory of positive thinking; how focusing on your positive thoughts makes a difference in how you respond to the challenges in your life.

"There is a basic law that like attracts like.
Negative thinking definitely attracts negative results.
Conversely, if a person habitually thinks optimistically and
hopefully, his positive thinking sets in motion creative forces
and success instead of eluding him, flows toward him."
~ Norman Vincent Peale ~

Scientific studies have reported that what we think affects our brain chemistry. When affirmations (negative or positive) are repeated either deliberately or by habit, they become implanted in your mind. If we think thoughts of stress our brain reacts to that thought in our body, and gives us additional similar thoughts. Additional studies indicated that stress affirmations negatively affect our self perception and self esteem, and positive affirmations can provide long term benefits to our self perception and self esteem.

Your subconscious mind cannot differentiate between actual reality and your affirmations, negative and positive. Just as your subconscious mind cannot differentiate between your anticipation of a stressful event and the actual event so it processes the affirmations as being real and this subconscious belief effects your nervous system. When you affirm stressful and hopeless thoughts, what you will then experience in your daily life will be stressful and feel hopeless. If your world seems to be falling around on top of you and very little if anything seems to be going your way, it can be insulting for someone to tell you that you should *"just think positive"* and everything will be better. It's not easy to think positive or see solutions when your life looks bleak and your energy is low. Later in this chapter are a few simple exercises to help change your affirmations from negative to positive.

Not everyone believes that thinking or saying positive affirmations can make any difference. Positive thinking will make very little if any difference if you only think positively on occasion or when you desperately trying to magically create a miracle. Research conducted by neuroscientists at NASA confirmed that it takes the brain 28 days to accept a change, and these research results support the theory we have heard for many years that it takes 3 weeks to change or make a habit. Additional NASA research also indicated that it is *essential* that the 28 days be consecutive without any breaks; and when a day was missed, all progress was lost and the day count had to start again at day one. In order for your brain to accept new programming, the input has to be everyday, for a minimum of 28 consecutive days, without exception.

In short, positive affirmations are a way to change your thoughts from fear and stress, to possibility and creative positive thinking; and by consistently practicing your affirmations, you will clear a path through the darkness of your stress to illuminate the ideas and solutions you have been seeking.

Louise Hay is renowned for being the Guru of affirmations. She began teaching about the power of affirmations after using them in her own life with resounding success. She had been through many life challenges since childhood and including a cancer diagnosis as an adult; all this led her to look for solutions for her life. She found strength and healing in changing her thoughts and the words she spoke. I feel fortunate to have met her in Hollywood over 25 years ago. Her peaceful self confidence and glowing health was part of her attraction and confirmation that she personally practiced what she preached.

Most likely the stressful statements you are affirming are not new visitors to your mind. Many of them came with luggage and have been settled in for quite some time. You are so accustomed to having them as your automatic reaction, that you may erroneously believe it's "just who you are". You must first be mindful of your statements; then be willing to let go of the old habitual way of verbally reacting and thinking and put a dedicated effort into affirmations. That is the only way to see how they will work for you.

Positive affirmations will make only a limited difference in your life, if you sit and think positive affirmations all day and never take any action towards any solution to change the situation or events that are causing you stress. Positive affirmations are the start of the change.

ℚᴛ Cost of stressful affirmations

Over 60% of people who visit their doctors and health care professionals every year are complaining about stress-related illnesses and pains. The mindfulness chapter covers a couple of exercises to show you how to be more observant and aware, yet the most obvious and most ignored is not external, it's internal – what we think and say. Even with all the evidence that stress kills, it can contribute to excess body weight, irritability, foggy thinking, migraines, heart disease and even cancer, some people are still not able to see the cost in their lives.

A visual three day exercise that can connect a cost factor to your thoughts can be done easily by using quarters.

Before you begin, go to the bank and get at least two rolls of quarters. When you run out of quarters, during this exercise, go back to the bank and get additional rolls. Keep these quarters in your pocket or in a pouch in your purse so they are very handy.

FIRST DAY: The minute that you hear yourself think or verbally say one of your stress statements, take a quarter from your collection and throw this quarter away, into the street.

➢ Throw it so you can hear it hit the ground.
➢ Watch it being tossed away.
   And leave it there.
➢ Every time you think or say a negative, energy draining stressful statement, throw away another quarter.

➢ DO NOT put these quarters in a jar to deposit into your bank account, or give to a charity. (Leaving the quarter on the ground, someone else who needs it may find it, so in that way you are being charitable. This exercise is to give you a physical and visual tool to see how costly your negative, stressful statements are.

➢ At the end of the day, calculate how expensive your stressful statements cost you, just in quarters.

SECOND DAY: Start with a count of how many quarters you have remaining from day one.

➢ **Today**, the minute that you hear yourself think or verbally say one of your stress statements, take a quarter from your collection and throw this quarter away, into the street.

➢ Throw it so you can hear it hit the ground.

➢ Watch it being tossed away.

➢ **This time** – as you look at your quarter on the ground, say a rephrased positive affirmation six times (read section on rephrase), then pick up your quarter and put it back into your pocket.

This step is to give you a physical and visual tool to see how you can change the effect of your negative, stressful statements.

➢ At the end of the day, calculate how many quarters you have remaining compared to what you started with.

THIRD DAY. Start with a count of how many quarters you have remaining from the previous two days.

➢ **Today** , the minute that you hear yourself think or verbally say one of your stress statements, take a quarter from your collection and WHILE YOU ARE STILL HOLDING ONTO IT, make a choice – (1) immediately say a rephrase affirmation six times, or (2) throw the quarter into the street, watching and hearing it leave your possession.

> ➤ If you rephrased, put your quarter back into your pocket.
> ➤ If you didn't rephrase and instead threw the quarter away, take another quarter from your collection and throw it away as well.
> ➤ **Each time** you start to think or say a negative stressful statement, you choose one of these same actions.
> ➤ At the end of the day, calculate how many quarters you still have compared to what you started with.

> *"Using quarters really woke me up to how much my old affirmations were costing me. I didn't want to do this exercise, but I made the agreement with myself I would follow it for three days. Halfway through my third roll of quarters, I really got serious about making changes. If I had kept my old affirmations, I would be in terrible financial trouble. I still carry quarters, and every time I see a quarter anywhere, I now remember to choose positive affirmations.. Thank you. "* ~ Pat Mynor ~

"Most folks are about as happy as they make up their mind to be."
~ Abraham Lincoln ~

QT   **A quick exercise – sensing how your words feel**
Before you begin to start making positive affirmations, it helps to have a feeling reference that you can personally recognize.

Take a minute to do this quick exercise:

Take one of your stressful statements, such as "this is hopeless" and say it only once. For most people their body will reflect a feeling of hopeless, droopy arms, slouched shoulders, lowered head and lowered voice. What is your body stance and feelings?

Now say – **louder** - *"This is a temporary setback, there is a solution."* And repeat it 6 times, each time making you voice louder.

As you do this, do you notice any change in how you are sitting or standing? Did you make any adjustments in your body, even if you didn't plan on it? Even if the shift in your body, you first attributed as being merely a fidget?

When most people effectively incorporate affirmations into their conversations with themselves and others, they notice they start to feel more confident, more hopeful and more tuned in to solutions and opportunities. Even if the solution hasn't arrived yet, we are more likely to recognize and be able to act on it when we are feeling hopeful and confident.

"Believing there is a solution paves the way to a solution."
~ Dr. David Schwartz ~

A clearer understanding

To more clearly understand how your stressful thoughts are affecting you, your body and emotions this exercise requires you to spend more time sensing specific areas of your body and emotions:

1. For this exercise you need a pen and a few pieces of clean paper.

2. Draw a line down the center of the page from top to bottom. On the left side, write 5 statements that you are affirming everyday about your stress and your view of your stress.

3. Write these statements in the left aide of your paper. These could be similar to the ones I mentioned at the beginning of this chapter, or you could have some that are more specific to your reactions about stress.

4. When you are finished writing your five stressful statements, set this paper aside. Take out a clean sheet

of paper and write the answers to these questions.

- ❖ Are you breathing fully or shallow?
- ❖ How does your solar plexus, your tummy area feel?
- ❖ How does your back feel?
- ❖ Do you feel comfortable or uncomfortable?
- ❖ Where are your eyes focused, straight head or looking down?
- ❖ Are you trembling or feeling solid?
- ❖ Are you standing or sitting tall or slumping?

This is now your reference as to how you feel the energy in your body when you are feeling stress, and focusing on your stressful thoughts and statements.

Put this paper aside; stand up, stretch and take in a few deep breaths.

Rephrase stress to a positive affirmation

5. Now go back to your paper with the 5 stressful statements. On the right hand side of this paper, across from each stressful statement, reword the stressful statement to a positive declaration without the word stress in the phrase. It is important that the rephrase be a positive statement as if it were already true in your life.

   An example might be:
   "I cannot handle this (_____) now becomes:
   "I am capable of handling whatever shows up in my life"
   or "I am capable of seeing creative solutions in my life"
   or "I have faith that I will always be ok."

6. Rephrase each of your stressful statements and then set your paper aside again.

7. Take out a new clean sheet of paper and write the answers to these questions as you think about your 5 rephrased, positive statements.

❖ Are you breathing fully or shallow?
❖ How does your solar plexus, your tummy area feel?
❖ How does your back feel?
❖ Do you feel comfortable or uncomfortable?
❖ Where are your eyes focused, straight head or looking down?
❖ Are you trembling or feeling solid?
❖ Are you standing or sitting tall or slumping?

For most people their body is tense and their breathing is shallow when they are focusing on their negative statements; and their body feels more relaxed when they are affirming the positive. So many people say that if one door closes another one opens, but you need to close the door on negative statements in order for the door of positive rewards to open. Many proponents of affirmations recommend that to outweigh a negative statement, a positive affirmation needs to be stated immediately and repeated at least six times. The more practice you give to saying the positive affirmations, the more you will feel the positive energy in your body, and your thoughts that follow.

A few other positive affirmations to get you started:

"I am stronger than I used to give myself credit for."
"I am surrounded by unlimited spiritual power that assists me in my solutions."
"Peacefulness is in my body more and more every day."
"I have many options."
"I can stay calm under pressure."

Write any of these on the right hand side of your paper, and any others that come to mind and that inspire you. Then rip the paper down the center line and throw the left side (the stressful statements) into the trash. This way you only have the positive statements to look at.

Your personal affirmations work best when they fit your life and your situation. Your circumstances and events are different that someone else's, so general affirmations work well to start until you can create affirmations that fit your personality and your life.

Sometimes the answer is a question

Sometimes stressful statements are difficult to rephrase so when that occurs, changing them into a question can be very beneficial. Stress statements can stop your from seeing a solution, whereas questions prompt creative thinking. "I can't handle this!" or "This is impossible! Can be changed to *"How* can I handle this?" or *"How* is this possible?"

When you have difficulty turning your stress statement into a positive affirmation, take a minute to do this quick exercise

1. Start by taking a minute to breathe and relax. Simple breathing exercise can be found in the chapter titled Breathe.

2. On a clean sheet of paper, turn it horizontal and divide it into three sections by drawing two separate lines from top to bottom.

3. On the left section, write the stressful statement you are having difficulty in rephrasing into a positive.

4. In the center section of the page, write the statement as a question.

5. As you continue to breathe and relax, write whatever solutions pop into your mind. Refrain from judging them at this time; simply write whatever comes into mind.

The first solutions may or may not be viable solutions; however, this exercise is to allow your creative ideas free space to create solutions.

This exercise may bring you a positive affirmation instead of a solution that you can act on. Either answer takes you from stress thinking to possibility and solution thinking so you can create your affirmations. Rip the far left section from the page and throw it away. If you have an answer to your question, discard the middle section of your page as well. Only keep the solutions or the positive statements so you can turn them into positive affirmations.

> *"Become a possibilitarian.*
> *No matter how dark things seem to be or actually are,*
> *raise your sights and see possibilities;*
> *always see them, for they're always there."*
> ~ Norman Vincent Peale ~

ℚⱦ   Getting the most benefit from your positive affirmations

1. Keep only your sheets of the positive affirmations.
2. Write your positive affirmations on sticky notes and attach to your mirror, your computer screen and anywhere you will see them on a regular basis.
3. Read each positive affirmation aloud, 6 times, everyday when you wake in the morning and again before you go to sleep at night.

4. Repeat your affirmations every for 30 days to establish a new habit of behavior and thinking.

> *"People often say that motivation doesn't last.*
> *Well, neither does bathing, that's why we recommend it daily."*
> ~ Zig Ziglar ~

Whenever you feel a stress thought creeping into your mind, convert it to a positive affirmation and repeat it 6 times. If you still feel stressed, repeat your affirmation another 6 times, or until you begin to feel less stressed. You can read a positive affirmation from your paper or nearest sticky note or create a brand new one.

The important part of affirmations is that they must be a positive statement, not a negative statement. A statement that would still be stressful would be "I need to feel peaceful." A positive statement instead is, "I am feeling more peaceful with every breath"

Affirmations require constant use in order to work. Stressful thoughts and fears are very powerful, and they need a more powerful antidote. Affirmations can be that cure, but only if you practice them often; repeating them daily whether you feel like it or not. Consistently repeating your positive affirmations with passion and eventually belief, will become your automatic response to stress.

"Every thought brings into action certain physical tissue, parts of the brain, nerve or muscle. This produces an actual physical change in the construction of the tissue. Therefore it is only necessary to have a certain number of thoughts on a given subject in order to bring about a complete change in the physical organization of a person."
~Charles Haanel ~

The little engine that could!

The following story of the little engine has been told and retold many times over the years and it shows how a little engine, met with a difficult task was able to stay motivated with a positive affirmation; which then turned into a statement of positive accomplishment.

A little railroad engine was employed at a station yard. Because of its size it was expected to only pull occasional small train cars. Also in the yard were large engines which were built for big and heavy hauling jobs.

One morning when the little engine was waiting for its next assignment a long train of freight-cars, filled with toys, pulled into the station. It asked the largest engine to pull it over the hill, so it could deliver its toys to children in the next town. "I can't; that is too much for me," said the largest and strongest engine. Then the train asked another engine, and another, only to hear the same excuse and refusals to even try. In desperation, the freight train looked around the train yard for any hope and saw the little engine. It asked the little engine if it would accept the job to pull it up the grade and down on the other side.

Without thinking twice the little engine puffed his response, "I think I can", and set about to put itself in front of the great heavy train. When he did, all the larger engines in the train yard laughed at him. They told him that if they couldn't do it then surely he couldn't.

The little engine ignored them and headed for the hill, puffing "I think I can, I think I can, I think I can."

He started up the hill with all his might. As the hill became more difficult, he continued to puff, "I think I can, I think I can, I think I can.". He ignored the laughter and taunting still coming from the larger engines in the train yard.

As the little engine pulled on, it became more difficult to pull the heavy freight train up the hill, so the little engine puffed louder, "I think I can, I think I can, I think I can". He kept bravely puffing faster and faster, and with each puff, repeated, "I think I can, I think I can, I think I can."

As it neared the top of the grade, which had so discouraged the larger engines, the little engine began to go more slowly under the strain and stress; however, it still kept repeating,

"I--think--I--can, I--think--I--can." He kept his focus on his goal and didn't look back. He didn't notice that the laughter from the larger engines below was now quieter, and not just because he was farther away from them. They never believed he would make it this far, so their taunting was being quieted by their amazement.

The little engine eventually reached the top and then went joyfully down on the other side of the grade, with cheerful puffs billowing, "I thought I could, I thought I could."

HAVE FAITH

MEMO FROM GOD
To: YOU   Date: TODAY
From: THE BIG BOSS   Subject: YOU
Reference: LIFE

I am GOD. Today I will be handling all of your problems and replacing them with many things that you can feel grateful for.

Please remember that I do NOT need your help. If life happens to deliver a situation to you that you fell that you cannot handle, no need for you to stress. Kindly put it in the SFGTD (something for God to do) box.

Your job is to enjoy life.

I can be a guilty of this as the next person – You pray to God (your Source, Universe, Spirit, Higher Power, your Religious or Spiritual Deity) to fix something that you need help to handle. Then - sometime later (moments for some), you interfere. You start to mentally discuss or fume how to handle it; worry it won't be taken care of; anxious it's not happening fast enough and you pick it up right where you left it off when you prayed, and sometimes you add more baggage when you pick it up.

Think for a moment if you went to the dentist you trusted with a toothache. You ask the doctor to fit it and take away the pain. Then the minute the dentist prepared to get started, you tell her what drill to use, how long the procedure should take; and halfway through the work, you take the drill from the dentist hand and proceed to do the job yourself. Sounds silly doesn't it.

If you gave a trusted friends or associate a project, and you REALLY had faith and trusted that this person was the most capable person to do this project, would you interfere? (If you are a Type A that can't delegate or let go, you might benefit from the chapter on Coaching & Counseling) For most people, when you believe that you gave the project to the most capable and trustworthy person to handle, you let it go. You relinquish control over how it's done, and trust that it will be done.

Faith is defined as: *confident belief in the trustworthiness of a person.* Your reaction to stress may be a time for you to revisit your faith.

> Faith in your spiritual or religious beliefs
> Faith in yourself
> Faith in others
> Faith in the eventual outcome

One of my favorite affirmations which points to faith, was in a greeting card I read over 10 years ago. It was written by Barbara J. Winter for Gibson Greetings:

"When you come to the edge
of all the light that you know,
And you are about to step off into the darkness
of the unknown,
Faith is knowing one of two things will happen:
There will be something solid to stand on
or you will be taught how to fly."

You can personalize this when you are unsure of what's next in your life: "As I step off into the unknown, I know there will be something solid to stand on or I will be taught how to fly."

This has helped me at time of stress, when the solution was in the dark unknown as are many solutions to the problems and events that cause us stress. The people I have shared this with have reported that regardless of what a person's religious or spiritual believe is, this affirmation seems to apply.

"If ye have faith as a grain of mustard seed,
ye shall say unto this mountain,
Remove hence to yonder placer; and it shall remove."
~ Holy Bible, King James Version ~

The cartoon on the next page was first discovered on the wall in a shipping department, with the caption *"you want it when"* to indicate that the request for a specific ship date was unthinkable. I've seen it used in numerous other business environments, and each time to represent that it was simply humorous to expect whatever the request was, to be fulfilled.

Years ago I changed the caption to: "**God can't do what?**" and "**My Source can't do what?**"

With **faith**, solutions are always possible.

God can't do what?
My Source can't do what?

Visit the website, www.stressout-book.com/stress-resources.htm to download a free copy of this graphic with your choice of "God" or "My Source"

QT **ERASE IT**

Wouldn't it be great to simply erase whatever it is that is causing you to feel stressed?

Using the creative visualization technique described in an earlier chapter visualize a chalk board in your minds eye. See the stressful event or the reoccurring fearful or stressful thought that keeps running through your mind on this screen.

See it clearly.

- ❖ Then see your hand holding a huge eraser.
- ❖ Use this eraser to erase the image on your mental screen.
- ❖ Run the eraser from right to left over and again until the image is completely erased.
- ❖ See you hand and the eraser traveling from left to right, and up and down over the entire screen image.

You can also move your hand physically in the air as you more it in your minds eye.

One therapist told me that the movement of your eyes from left to right as the image is being erased is a very important part of the process. This releases the energy you have attached to the event or thought. Another person who uses this technique said her coach told her that it was the movement of her physical hand as well as her mental hand together erasing the image that releases the emotional connection to the event or thought.

So even though it's not specific **how** it works, for the people I interviewed who use this technique, it *works*! Take out your big eraser and see for yourself.

CHECK YOUR LIST

One day I went out to have lunch by myself at a nice restaurant. Dining alone, on occasion, allows me time to watch the events around me, ponder and make notes. It was a nice day and my table was in the outside area where I could listen to the birds and watch the ducks in a nearby pond. When I was seated, the table had room enough for four, but the hostess seated me there anyway.

I sat for a while sipping tea and nibbling on bread before I decided I was hungry. As I was studying the menu, the hostess stopped by my table to inform me that the restaurant had suddenly become quite busy and wondered if I would be willing for two other women to share my table. It seemed like a simple request, so I agreed, and I was joined by two very pleasant women, Connie and Barbara. They asked that their last names not be included here.

After greeting each other and introducing ourselves, we seemed to ignore each other paying attention to our own business. When our meals arrived, and I removed my work from the table, Connie noticed the book cover and asked me what I was working on. After explaining my project, they were happy to share with me a tool they use. It was Connie's Mom who shared with them the Irish saying:

"Count your joys instead of your woes;
Count your friends instead of your foes."
~ Irish Saying ~

Many people can create lists of problems in their lives, but they have difficulty shifting their focus from the problems to the good things.

When they shared their list making exercise with me, I shared with them a Simple Key™ tool using a pencil and a black ink pen that might add to the impact of their exercise. They both agreed to use it and call me with their results.

A few days I received a call from Connie. She told me she did her lists again, this time using the pencil and black ink pen. She shared with me how differently this felt for her. Without any effort her eyes focused on the more predominant words, those written in the black ink.

The combined exercise

For this exercise, you will need a pencil and a black felt tipped marker, and a few clean sheets of paper. Draw a line vertically down the center of each paper forming two columns on each.

1. Using the pencil on one paper at the top of the left side column write WOES, and using the black felt tip marker, on the right side write JOYS.

2. On the second paper left side column, using the pencil, write FOES, and using the black felt tipped pen, on the right side column write FRIENDS at the top.

3. On the first sheet of paper, **using your PENCIL,** start writing down only your **WOES.** Let it out, only you will see this list. Keep writing until you have run out of statements to write.

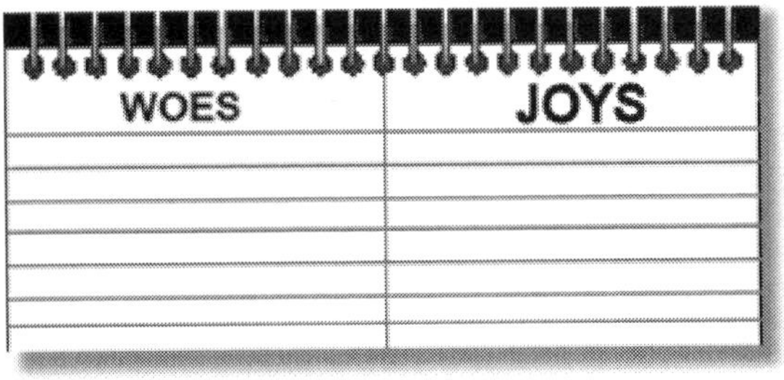

4. When you have written all your woes, take out your second sheet of paper where you have written Foes and Friends.
5. Under the **FOES** header, **using your PENCIL**, name all those people who you feel are against you, don't like you, are standing in your way or in some way you feel they are contributing to a difficult situation and stress in your life. Keep writing until you have run out of names to write under your Foes column.

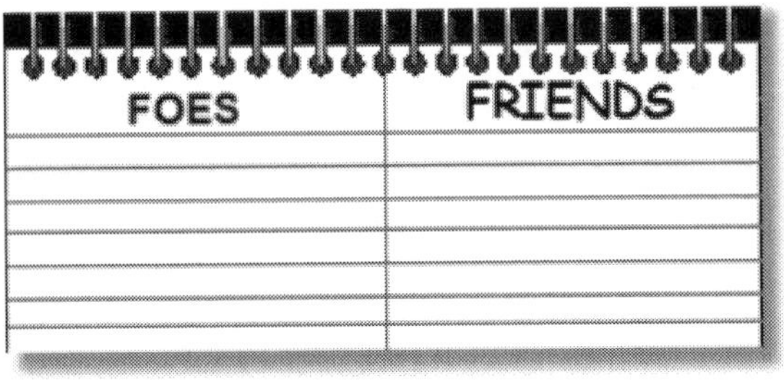

6. When you are finished writing your lists of woes and foes, put down your pencil and stand up. Stand tall, with your feet placed approximately hip width apart and take in a very deep breathe and open your arms wide to your side horizontal with the ground. Look up; tilt your head back and stretch, opening your chest.

   Breathe in deeply and exhale slowly. Do this three times. Then sit down and continue to breathe normally.

7. Now pick up the **BLACK INK PEN** and on the right side column of the first list, start writing your **JOYS**. Write **LARGE**. If you find you need more room to write, overwrite your entries in the left side woes column.

   While you are doing this, be aware of your breathing and continue to breathe fully with the support of your diaphragm. Keep writing until you have run out of statements to write.

8. After you have finished with your list of **JOYS**, set this list aside and pick up your second list and write the names of each of your **FRIENDS**. If you find you need more room to write, overwrite your entries in the foes column.

An important note here: If you find that your Friends or Joys list is shorter, don't let yourself become concerned. When you are feeling stressed, you may have a temporary clouded memory of your joys and friends.   Plus it's important to remember that the quality of a genuine friend equals much more than an assortment of acquaintances and fair weather friends. A single $1000 bill has more value than 1000 pennies and a gallon of juice has more nutrients than 100 teaspoons of juice. This is not to suggest there is something wrong with wanting a fan club. What is really being addressed here is accepting the value in the friends you have in your life.

"But friendship is the breathing rose, with sweets in every fold."
~ Oliver Wendell Holmes ~

9. When you are finished writing your lists of JOYS and FRIENDS, set these lists aside. Observe how you feel after you finish writing your lists of Joys and Friends.

For most people their body is tense and their breathing is shallow when they are writing their list of woes and foes. On the other hand, when they finish writing their Joys and Friends list in larger letters, they feel large. They feel happier. And when you are feeling happy, it is difficult to feel stressed. Your body tissue and muscles have memory like your brain. Current research reports show that feeling happier and focusing on love and joy can actually change the chemistry of your brain. The more often and longer you let yourself feel the feelings that you felt when you write your Joys and Friends lists, the easier it will be to recall them when you need to shift your energy from stress.

Excerpt from The "G" spot = the ecstasy of life through GRATITUDE (see resource section for more details about this book)

CHANGE THE CHANNEL

"We must also be careful to avoid ingesting toxins
in the form of violent TV programs,
video games, movies, magazines, and books.
When we watch that kind of violence,
we water our own negative seeds, or tendencies,
and eventually we will think and act out of those seeds. "
~ Thich Nhat Hahn ~

The movies and television shows you watch have influence over your stress level. If what you are feeling is stressed and anxious, and you watch a movie that is violent, or the depressing segments of the news, you are reducing your ability to choose a positive response to your stress.

Alternatively, when you are feeling overwhelmed, stressed, unable to think clearly, or when you just need a break - watch a short inspiration movie, or comedy. Fifteen minutes of inspiration, or something that motivates you to laugh makes everything much easier after that. This is better than a long movie where if you watch only 15 minutes, your mind stays with the movie wondering what's next, instead of being able to focus on your task at hand.

There are a few places where you can find short movies to give you that 15 minute distraction:

The Internet – In a few minutes you can find dozens of short videos on a mirage of topics on YouTube. Simply bookmark your favorites. Networks are now posting their weekly shows episodes online. These episodes usually have commercials every few minutes however; so you can watch the episode in segments or distract yourself during the commercials.

Online auction sites and local discount stores – I found a collection of old black/white movies in a discount store. Some of these were old comedy shows on CD and they were only $1 each. I loved these shows when I was a kid and now I can watch them again. On e-Bay and Amazon auction you will find a variety of movies, old and new. Find the ones that you can watch when you need that break, and then when you are done with the movie, put them back online for sale.

Monthly DVD clubs. A few select clubs, such as Spiritual Cinema Circle offer not only full length movies, but their subscriptions include inspirational shorts as well. With other online movie rental clubs, you can select some of your favorite funny sitcoms and without the commercials, the full episode runs in much shorter time.

TV – set your TIVO, DVR or video recorder to record your favorite comedy shows whose jokes are easy to listen to and those that create positive emotions. Stay away from comedy that demeans or attacks any group, and instead find shows that help you to laugh at life. Record these shows and when you need a laugh or a quick pick me up, simply watch 10-15 minutes. It can do the trick.

When you are fast forwarding through your recorded shows, don't focus on the quickly passing ads. Your rapid eye movement as you focus on these rapidly changing scenes can cause you to retain some of the messages in the ads. Marketing companies spend billions to get you to react and buy their products and they take into consideration societies changing viewing habits when they choose images and content. This is evident in the many people who rush to buy the latest gadget, outfit, beauty supply, automobile. In the Get Moving chapter you will find an old fashioned tip of something to do during these commercials.

Plan ahead and start collecting short segments so you have something fun and positive to focus on when you need to take a break.

MINDFULNESS

Mindfulness is being fully present, in each moment of your life, and being aware in all your experiences. Being mindful allows you to be open to new information; it is listening to your inner voice, your body signals and using this information to consciously make your choices.

Mindfulness is being willing to stop, think and question your premature cognitive commitments. Simply stated mindfulness means to pay full attention to what you are doing, moment by moment. In his books, Eckhart Tolle called it "being in the now."

Unfortunately many people go through life robotically, and reactively. When the stressful events in their life show up and they feel unprepared or underequipped so they react with old habits and unhealthy methods.

Some of our habits were developed in younger years and we made *premature cognitive commitments* to them. Our mindlessness has been was developed throughout our life without ever questioning ourselves, whether these "habits", "opinions" and "behaviors", are helping us or hurting us.

We live in a physical world that is consumed with moving forward before we have visited today. When I was a child emphasis was placed on Thanksgiving the week of Thanksgiving and Christmas decorations were not seen until the first of December. Now days, you see Christmas decorations next to Easter decorations. You see Christmas trees being erected in malls before Thanksgiving. When you want to buy a winter sweater, you have to shop in the heat of summer, because the retail stores are showing bathing suits in winter.

We spend so much time planning our goals and our future that our life seems to rush by. Do you go with the flow and play a part in the symphony of the crowd, or do you stay with the song of your own drummer and take each day as you choose it, regardless of what the crowds are doing? Either way is right - as long as you are mindful of your choices.

Mindfulness is responding rather than reacting to life. Mindfulness is living from full involvement in each in each moment of our life which makes it easier to choose our responses, rather than mindless knee-jerk reactions.

When operating their lives in mindfulness, researchers have reported that some people find it easier to take risks or be more comfortable with change. Many have felt less fearful of failure, which has opened their doors wider for success. They have found that weight and stress are easier to manage with Mindfulness, and all their major relationships are more fulfilling.

Excellent examples of mindfulness in action are athletes. They are mindful of every stage of their training, their movements and their goals. The more mindful their focus, the more often they reach and exceed their goals. At the 2008 Olympics, Michael Phelps broke all records in the water. In interviews he talked about how he stayed clear and focused every minute on his goals, and his actions with every stroke in the water.

When we live mindlessly, we miss some of the valuable information that is directly in front of us including the solutions to our stress.

In 1999 Daniel Simons at the University of Illinois Video Cognition Lab created a video that has circulated the internet, has been shown and referenced in numerous presentations to help people to recognize how unaware they are in their observations.

The people watching the video are given one instruction: to count a certain number of times a basketball is passed from one person to another. After the video is done, they are asked only one question which tested their mindful observations — and the majority of viewers answered incorrectly.

They did not see an activity taking place that was very obvious when they were told it was there, and they saw the video the second time. It was so obvious that nearly everyone questioned how they could have missed it the first time. The link to the video and the instructions are in the resource section of this book. So many people go through life only seeing portions of their reality.

Whatever we focus on mindfully in life, we will see with more clarity. We either see problems or solutions.

Mindfulness is being fully present, in each moment of your life, and being aware and observant of all your choices, opinions, judgments and experiences. Mindfulness is listening to your inner voice, your body signals and using this information to consciously make your choices. Mindfulness is listening and paying attention to your life, your choices and your responses to the events in your life. Mindfulness is being willing to stop, think and question the premature cognitive commitments you made early in life and your habits.

West Virginia University and the University of California Los Angeles tested the effects of mindfulness techniques on stress and in both studies they concluded that mindfulness exercises are excellent stress-busters. The goal of the study was to relieve stress. The participants were taught how to recognize sources of stress, how stress impacts them, and then what they could do to come out of the vicious cycle of stress reactivity. The lead investigator said, when done correctly, mindfulness brings awareness to the body that normally is always being rushed and results showed that mindfulness can actually lift stress from your body.

As a baby you were mindful of everything in your life. It was all you knew. We have since learned how to rush about and lose focus. When you are mindful you will notice when your shoulders or neck *starts* to tense up from stress, or you will recognize when you have been sitting at your desk non-stop for too long. Being mindful, you will observe how your body reacts to the food you eat, and the music you listen to and the words you use.

You can easily re-learn to be mindful in your life. These three simple exercises are only a few of the ways you can practice mindfulness.

Mindfulness exercises:

Breath

Mindful breathing can assist in putting an end to distracting thoughts and help you to stay focused and in the moment.

❖ For this mindful breathing exercise, sit comfortably and take in deep breaths through your nostrils.
❖ Feel the sensation.
❖ Take in deep breaths through your nose, and on the exhale, allow your air to flow through your lips. This should be simple and natural.
❖ Continue to take deep breaths and focus on the **sound** of your breath as you inhale and exhale.
❖ If your mind begins to wander, simply accept it without judgment, and then bring your focus back to the sound of your breath.
❖ Breathe into your lungs.
❖ Can you feel your chest expand without opening your eyes and looking at it?
❖ Breathe fully with the support of your diaphragm and let your body expand and relax with each breath.

❖ Can you sense the expansion of your tummy without having to open your eyes and look?

❖ Breathe purposefully and slowly and focus on the *sound* and *flow* of your breath.

❖ Continue for a few more breaths.

❖ Then allow yourself to breathe your usual breathing style.

❖ When you feel comfortable with your usual breathing style, open your eyes.

You have practiced one form of Mindful breathing by being in the moment with the sound and flow of your breath in each moment. You can practice this exercise anytime you need a quick shift in your focus.

Walking

Mindful walking is one of my favorite mindful exercises that I learned from Thich Nhat Hahn, a renowned Zen Buddhist Monk and teacher of mindfulness. This exercise requires you to be on dirt ground or grass. The movements in this exercise are slow and intentional.

❖ Remove your shoes and step barefooted onto the dirt or the grass. Feel the ground solidly under your feet.

❖ Sense your toes and what they feel.

❖ Sense your heel and what you feel on that part of your foot.

❖ Is your arch touching the ground or do you feel air between the arch of your feet and the ground.

❖ What is the temperature and texture you feel under each foot? Is what you sense, the same or different for each foot?

❖ Sense what you feel on the top of your foot. Is the temperature the same or different?

❖ Is there a breeze that you feel, or is the air still?

❖ When you have fully sensed this position, take one step forward. As your foot is lifted from the ground, sense the change in temperature and sensations on your foot, both top and bottom.

❖ When you set your foot on the ground, again focus on each feeling of touch under your foot.

❖ Is there any sound when you stepped down?

❖ Is the temperature the same or different than previously?

❖ Are your feet feeling the same textures as you did previously?

With each step, every time you sense the textures, sounds and temperature you are practicing being mindful in the moment.

If you were to watch every step you took, you would also notice colors and textures that you might have otherwise missed.

We take breathing and walking for granted. Taking the time to be mindful during these two exercises can change your perspective on other habits you take for granted.

Music

Listening to music many people automatically practice mindfulness without even realizing that is what they are doing.

❖ Put on one of your favorite songs.

❖ Close your eyes and listen.

❖ How many different notes can you distinguish?

❖ What parts of your body respond to the sounds besides your ears? Many people feel the sounds in their chest or their abdomen.

❖ If your music choice has words, do you hear words you didn't hear before?

❖ How do your body and your emotions respond to this music?

It is important not to become ambitious or to give yourself limits on what you need to or think you are supposed to experience. Allow yourself to remove the boundaries and limits and just be with the free space. This will take practice and patience with yourself, however, the rewards of mindfulness will be worth it.

Give yourself a gift of mindfulness.

For the next 7 days, participate in a mindfulness practice, once a day. Start by intentionally observing what you are doing.

❖ If you are working at your desk, pay attention to your thoughts as you handle paperwork, reach to answer the phone, answer emails and work on your projects.

❖ When you move away from your desk, be consciously aware of your feet on the carpet or bare floor and the muscles not only in your legs and feet, but also the muscles in your torso that are used then you walk. Observe your thoughts about where you are going. This second part has helped dieters become more aware of the mindless trips they take to the refrigerator.

❖ When you exercise, if you are a walker or runner, bring your attention to the feel and sound of your feet as they strike the ground. If you participate in an aerobic exercise, observe the specific muscles you are using, and listen to your thoughts and attitude while you make each move.

Give yourself 15 minutes to practice mindfulness.
Keep a journal of your thoughts and experiences.

Mindfulness can be practiced with any event, at any time. You may wonder how these exercises could make any difference in your stress and your ability to reduce your unhealthy stress reactions. Mindfulness put you in a place where you can gain perspective on everything you are doing at the moment Studies show that mindfulness can be helpful in recognizing your unhealthy automatic reactions to stress, and help you to control your thoughts, inner chatter and negative worries over things that cause you stress. When you are mindful, you will feel when your body starts to tense, or your stomach beings to churn or other stress reactions you have felt in your body, which gives you the opportunity to be proactive and relax instead. It can also be used to decrease your worry over the future and release guilt feelings from the past. The more you practice mindfulness, the easier it will become for you to focus on the present moments in your days and recognize your strengths, your capabilities and see solutions to your previously stressful reactive actions.

Look To This Day
For it is Life, the very Life of Life.
In Its brief course lie all the Verities and Realities of your existence;
The Bliss of Growth;
The Glory of Action;
The Splendor of Beauty;
For Yesterday is but a Dream,
And tomorrow is only a Vision:
But Today well lived makes every
Yesterday a Dream of Happiness,
and Every Tomorrow a Vision of Hope.
Look well, therefore, to This Day!
~ From the Sanskrit ~

ℚ𝕋 TO-DO or TA DAHS

So many people jump out of bed, to rush into their day and start handling whatever comes up as it happens. They complain that it's difficult and stressful, over and over again. With this behavior they are doing two things, affirming the stress in words, (See the chapter, What's on your Mind?) and mental images (see the chapter Creative Visualization).

Many people create a to-do list and start their day looking at this list that can then stimulate feelings of stress, and words and images of too much to do, and feelings of being overwhelmed.

Sandy shared with me that she writes a list, but her to-do list had things on it that she has already handled. This way she can go down her list and check things off; and seeing the check marks makes her feel good.

If you like making to-do lists, instead of simply listing what you have to do, make your to-do list with your positive outcomes and hopeful results – your **Ta-Dahs!** This way you are focusing on the excitement of your results instead of the stress of what you think you have to do.

Most people can be motivated in anticipation of a positive outcome. We have good feelings of accomplishments when we achieve a positive result and we want more of the same. Studies show that the best time for a salesperson to make a sale is right after you have made one. The best time to create other positive results in your life is right after you have just experienced one.

Date: _____

To Do   Ta -Dah!

✔
_____   _____
_____ ☐ _____
_____ ☐ _____

As you write your to-do list of what you feel you need to do, write next to each one, how you will feel when this result is achieved. This is your Ta-Dah feeling. See that image in your mind. Focus on that column of your to do list and it will help you to make your day full of Ta-Dah's

In the chapter, New Ways to Journal, you can read about the benefits of the daily accomplishment journal.

MEDITATION

Countless studies from researchers indicate that meditation is highly effective in reducing stress.

A study at a large corporation showed that employees who followed a regular Meditation practice, had reduced tension on the job.

A study of students practicing meditation showed a significant increase in their learning abilities.

Medical studies indicate that meditation decreases stress and decreases the stress hormone cortisol.

Meditation can slow down the chatter in your mind. The psychologist Carl Jung considered his meditation retreats essential to his well being, "Talking is a torment to me, and I need many days of silence to recover from the futility of words."

"No one can get inner peace by pouncing on it. "
~ Harry Emerson Fosdick ~

Many people define Meditation by the Webster dictionary which says, "to ponder, to reflect upon". For some the word meditation means contemplation and for others it means peace or empty mind, without thought. In all cases you are correct. Although these definitions can be meditation, it is also much more.

The term meditation actually refers to a group of techniques, such as mantra meditation, walking meditation, chants, transcendental meditation, relaxation response, mindfulness meditation, guided and visualization meditations, Zen Buddhist meditation, Yoga and Tai Chi and many others.

Paul Farrell, JD, PhD, in his book titled The Millionaire Meditation wrote about several types of meditation used by high performing executives on Wall Street. These included traditional sitting meditations, sports and fitness mediations, creativity and passionate meditation and relationship meditations such as mastermind groups, intimate relationship and parenting as meditation.

Meditation is awareness.

Meditation is quietly sitting and eliminating distractions.

Meditation is setting your mind on one thing.

Meditation is mindfulness.

Meditation is chanting.

Meditation is listening to your heartbeat.

Meditation is watching the sunrise or sunset.

Meditation is a simple way to deal with stress.

Meditation can calm your mind and your body.

Meditation is love.

Meditation can produce a greater overall sense of well-being.

Meditation brings about the union of opposites. Ying and Yang, your active and passive, your conscious mind, subconscious mind, your spiritual and your physical balance.

Meditation can assist you in achieving or receiving many benefits: mental, physical, emotional and spiritual.

Meditation can be a mirror reflection of your life, and Mindfulness allows you to look, see and make changes - deep inside, which can then change your outside world.

Meditation techniques have been used for centuries in many forms by many different cultures outside of traditional religious or cultural settings, for health and wellness purposes. Many religious and spiritual teachings include meditation as a way to communicate and listen for guidance. And meditation is used by countless people in non-religious settings. Stress has always been one of the reasons that people are resorting to meditation outside of a religious or spiritual setting.

There are several types of meditation. After you learn the techniques of meditation, you can do it on your own, in a class or a meditation group. Countless people start and end their days in mediation. Results from a study at John Hopkins Medical Center indicated that meditation was an effective treatment for reducing stress and anxiety that accompanies daily life

Meditation can be used with affirmations and prayer; by listening to music or the sounds of nature. Meditation can be applied to nearly every aspect of your life. Meditation is mentioned in several chapters in this book. In one chapter titled Honor Yourself, Nancy Miiller introduces you to a ceremony that includes meditation.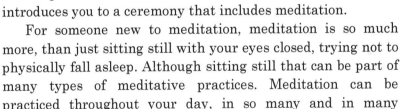

For someone new to meditation, meditation is so much more, than just sitting still with your eyes closed, trying not to physically fall asleep. Although sitting still that can be part of many types of meditative practices. Meditation can be practiced throughout your day, in so many and in many different activities.

The reasons given by most people who don't meditate:

1. Impatience, thinking that 10 minutes is too long or an impossible amount of time to sit still, even though some people can sit for hours in front of a computer screen or TV set without moving. With as little as ten minutes a day, in a short time you can see significant benefits in your physical and mental states.

2. Skepticism, thinking that meditation is simply zoning out and has no real value.

3. Don't know how. Meditation is simple to learn. Regardless of whether you can meditate for five minutes or fifty, there are many choices and types of meditation. Meditation classes are being offered in many community centers, through doctor's offices, special events, books and recordings.

The following are only a few of the available types of meditations which can be practiced anytime stress starts to creep in. Still, quiet meditations are best when you are sitting up, not laying down. When we lay down, flat on our back and relax, we are usually in bed ready for sleep. Your body responds to this habit, so if you lay down to meditate your chances of falling asleep are much greater. If you do fall asleep during a sitting meditation, you may need more actual sleep. Movement meditations are easiest when you are wearing the appropriate or loose fitting clothing.

Although the term Meditation covers a variety of techniques, the two most common are meditations focused on breathing and the repetition of a soothing word or phrase.

Mindful Meditation

A study conducted by the University of New Mexico which included mindful meditation showed that after 8 weeks the participants had significant improvement in their well-being, and ability to reduce perceived stress and depression. Mindful Meditation is being fully present, in each moment, and one of the great parts of this, is that you are already practicing mindfulness in some part of your life. Mindful meditation encourages you to become mindful of thoughts, feelings, and sensations and to observe them in a nonjudgmental way. Practicing mindful meditation can change how you relate to the flow of emotions and thoughts in your mind. You can practice Mindful Meditation while involved in movement as well, such as dancing or walking. The key is the *"Mindfulness"*. In active mindful meditation, you are experiencing all parts of life. Therefore both stillness and activity, and silence or sounds can be experienced in mindful meditation. By practicing Mindful Meditation, you experience the NOW. Mindful breathing, walking and mindfully listening to music was introduced in the Mindfulness chapter. Each of these can become a 10-30 minute meditation.

Zen Meditation

Zen meditation is also called the breath meditation and the purpose is to sit still, and empty your mind. Focusing on one thing and breathing

You can practice this meditation technique when you start to feel stress, or before you are approaching an event where you anticipate stress.

You will be counting each time you exhale, but only to 5. You will know your attention has wandered when you find yourself up to "eight," "ten" or more.

❖ Sit in a comfortable position, close your eyes and start with a few deep breaths. Then let your breath flow naturally without trying to control it. Ideally it will be quiet, deep and slow, but it will vary for each person.

❖ To begin the exercise, count to yourself as you exhale.

❖ Begin with "one", the second breath, count "two" and continue with each breath up to "five."

❖ On your sixth breath, start again at number one, and with each following breath count again up to five.

❖ After you have counted to five a few times, take in a deep breath and then open our eyes.

Most people find themselves in a more relaxed state after just a few minutes of Zen.

Mantra or Chant Meditations

Similar to Transcendental Meditation this type of meditation uses repetition of a word or sound as a focal point. The Mantra (phrase) is repeated throughout the meditation and all your thoughts are focused on the Mantra.

Transcendental Meditation® was formed by Maharishi Mahesh Yogi. People practicing TM are usually given their mantra by their TM teacher. In your personal mantra meditation, you can choose a special word, such as love or peace or one with special meaning to you and repeat it effortlessly and continuously during your meditation.

QT Calming Meditation
This meditation can be practiced immediately anytime you begin to feel stress.

❖ Close your eyes and begin breathing, slow purposeful breaths.

❖ Breathe in through your nose and without stopping, exhale through your mouth.

❖ Focus on your breathe and the continuous flow of inhale and exhale.

❖ After a few calming breaths, open your eyes.

Calming meditation can also be practiced with your eyes open when you are driving or in a group setting. Most people won't notice that you aren't paying attention to them for a minute while you are focusing on breathing calmly.

Releasing Meditation
Releasing stress using words can be combined with the calming meditation.

On the inhale say a calming word to yourself such as love or peace, and on the exhale, exhale the word stress, or anger, or frustration. Whatever fits that moment. You can add creative visualization to your words by seeing "peace and love" coming to you and "stress" leave you. You can include mindfulness and feel and sense the stress leave your body and energy, and be replaced with love and peace.

Guided Meditations.

With Guided meditation a teacher guides your thought process. On the topic of guided meditation, a popular question arises regarding the difference between hypnosis, self hypnosis, guided imagery and creative visualization. Each of these gives you suggestions of images to see and experience. In hypnosis, guided imagery or guided meditations someone other than yourself is giving you the instructions. In self hypnosis and creative visualizations, you are using your words and energy to create the images and your responses. Exercises in the Creative Visualization chapter can be used to increase your ability to see the suggested images in guided meditations.

There are several other types and variations of meditation, which allows you the opportunity to find one that works for you. As you practice Meditation, wonderful changes can happen in your day. Your inner perspective increases and you start to see things in a different light. Your confidence continues to build and your capability expands, and by doing so, you change your stress responses.

Meditation can be practiced almost anywhere. It is possible to meditate on your own. With a group, you may find the group energy can be helpful especially when you first begin to learn and practice meditation.

For most people new to meditation, having audio guidance is helpful. Links to free audio and video meditations will be posted on the Stress Out website.

"We have been accustomed to thinking that we have to get something from outside of us in order to be happy, but in truth it works the other way: We must learn to contact our inner source of happiness and satisfaction and flow it outward to share with others – not because it is virtuous to do so, but because it feels really good!"
~ Shakti Gawain ~

CREATIVE VISUALIZATION

Visualization is a technique you can use whether you are awake and asleep. You visualize when you "think ahead" about an event or activity and you form a mental image of whatever you are anticipating. In your sleep, you visualize images in your dreams. Some dreams can seem so real that when you wake, you have a little initial confusion as you attempt to discern if it was a dream or if it was real.

Visualization is used in guided meditations, hypnosis and self hypnosis. Creative visualization is different than simple daydreaming. Creative visualization is seen through your minds eyes in full detail using all of your five senses. When all 5 senses are involved, your ideas (whether stress or opposite) becomes more enhanced and real. Your subconscious mind easily understands pictures.

With creative visualization you see yourself in another place, a place where your stress leaves you. This can not only shift your stress energy, but it can also stimulate your creative thinking, which brings you solutions that you can then put into action.

With creative visualization you are seeing the image through your eyes, not watching it on a screen somewhere in front of you. Instead of watching the image, you are feeling it, sensing it, seeing it, touching it and hearing it. All of your senses are engaged. The key is to see the picture vividly real in your mind, through your own eyes. The more connected your five senses are to your image, the more real it will feel. The more real you feel it, the more it affects your attitude and daily life in a positive, powerful way.

"See things as you would have them be instead of as they are."
~ Robert Collier ~

Let go of people that aggravate you

Barbara Kramer says that seems like nearly everyday, when she's working on a deadline, that someone seems to get in her way. She uses creative visualization when she feels that someone is really getting on her nerves.

She takes a minute and closes her eyes, takes a very deep, slow breath and vividly imagines herself sitting at the side of a beautiful flowing stream of cool water. She then continues her visualization as she sees herself walk into the stream and splash around in the water. She vividly senses the feeling of the cool water on her legs and feet. At this point she can actually physically feel her stress begin to leave her. In her visualization she vividly sees the beautiful scenery, the open sky and all the beauty around her.

She invites the person who has been aggravating her to show up next to her at the stream. She sees a small boat tied up next to her at the bank of the stream. She invites this person to get into the boat, and after watching him do this, she sees her hands untie the rope, letting the boat travel downstream with the flow, taking this person and their behavior farther away from her.

As the boat fades from her mental view, she is not longer feeling any attachment to the feelings of aggravation she started out with.

Barbara explains that her intent is never to see harm inflicted on another person, but this creative visualization releases her from the stress she feels in her reaction to the other person's behavior. She then continues her visualization with vividly seeing herself being productive and finishing her project sooner than her deadline. She feels her confidence and feelings of a job well done. She can taste the ice cream she will reward herself with when the job is complete. Now her stress reactions are no longer in her mind or in her body. When she opens her eyes and starts back to work she can handle what is happening in the real life situation with more ease.

Focus on what you can control

When I first began planning my wedding, thoughts of what I wanted and was afraid might go wrong dominated my mind. I had appointments throughout my workday for meetings and decisions related to my wedding, so even though this was a joyous event, I was stressed. Every bride to be knows about the juggling of wedding planning with their work and other personal commitments. I was stressed about what I wanted for this much very special day; stressed about what could go wrong; stressed about the cost; and stressed because I was feeling so stressed!

I went to bed at night with these thoughts and fears and woke up in the morning picking up where I left off. I was tired, because I hadn't slept peacefully.

Fortunately I sought help. The advices I heard and practiced make a huge difference in my stress level and my enjoyment when the day arrived.

I started by writing a detailed picture of my perfect wedding day. I focused on the people, the joy, the laughter and the enthusiasm. I wrote in detail how I wanted the day to be, focusing on my five senses. Although in my description of my wedding, I wore a beautiful white dress, I wrote more about how I felt in that dress than how the dress looked. I wrote about how much my guests enjoyed the wedding and the mingling with each other, rather than focusing on the food or the entertainment.

Each evening, even though I felt I was as organized as I could be during the day, I needed to let go of that list I kept in my head before I went to bed. I started by writing two lists, one of everything that was bothering me, and another list of what I needed to do, my still to-do list. I made two separate lists so I didn't need to look at the "bothering me" list again. The "to-do" list had the phone calls to make, the agreements to sign, the site visits, the friends I needed to connect with and it also included anything I could delegate. I then put these two lists on my desk to be left alone until the next day.

Now that my mind could be relieved of these "must remembers", I needed to fill that space with something else or those thoughts would jump back in again. I began by turning off the TV and turning on peaceful music, something with water sounds and no vocals. I lit my favorite fragrance candles and read from books that I had preselected to be available. These were poetry, humor and inspirational stories. And just before going to bed, I would read the description I had written of my perfect wedding and feel the *feelings* I had described.

When I awoke in the morning, before getting out of bed, I reread and replayed that description of my perfect wedding in my mind. After than, when I got up and started my day, I started with a joyous feeling, not a feeling of stress or worry.

During my day, I also found it helpful when I started to stress over the tasks related to my wedding, I would read my perfect wedding day description and focus on the feelings. Most women have a dream of what their wedding should be like. We have all heard, and now there's even a television show, of horror stories how bride-to-be's became bridezillas - stressed out over the dress, the flowers, the location, etc. I wanted to remember my wedding day by the feelings not the stress or any problems.

I kept this routine up to the day of my wedding. Did anything go wrong that day? Yes, things I couldn't have anticipated. My hairdresser was late to arrive to style my hair, which made me late to the ceremony. While our guests waited for me to arrive at the beautiful outside location, a small swarm of bees came to visit. My dress didn't fit, two of my sisters got upset with me, the main course was bland, and I wasn't stressed. I got the giggles during my vows and had difficulty regaining my composure and everyone giggled with me. Also unexpected was the rooster who wasn't on the guest list, who showed up just as I turned the corner to enter the patio area. He strutted ahead of me on the path, announcing me with each step. And the butterflies that hovered over the alter area during our vows. Even writing this now I have a smile on my face because I remember how good I felt that day.

5 Minutes to Lower Stress

"After being a stay-at-home Mom for 18 years I finally landed a good assistant position in a large firm across town. Soon after I started this new job, I started to get consistent stress migraines. I was so concerned about forgetting something every time I left the house, and I worried about it all the way to work. I was in a state of constant stress. When I had a stress migraine I had to stop everything and go to bed because I could no longer think, or move or do anything. I was afraid I might lose my new job. After being at home for so many years, I was afraid I might be forgetting to feed the pets, or turn something off, or forget to lock something on my rush to work. I read about creative visualizing and it made sense enough that I decided to give it a try. Now before leaving my house to go to work, I take 5 minutes to creatively visualize myself comfortably driving to work with the feeling of confidence that I have completed everything at home; that everything that should be locked, is locked; everything that should be turned off, is off; the animals are fed, and so on; including that I am wearing the appropriate outfit to the office. I have been doing this now for 6 months, and have not had any of my usual stress migraines. My boss is happy that I no longer miss so many days from work and I find myself enjoying the drive to work listening to my favorite music instead of worrying." ~ *Julie Cucina* ~

Your existing creative ability

If you have never intentionally practiced creative visualization, you may think it is difficult or that you can't do it. To give your self an opportunity to see how creative your mind is, start with this exercise:

1. Find a place where you can be undisturbed for a few minutes. Sit comfortably in a chair, do not slouch.

2. Think about a friend and remember the last time you saw this person and had a conversation. See this memory in your mind. See your friend exactly as you saw them at that time. See the place where you were, any furniture or other items around you. Recall the conversation you were having with each other.

3. Now see this friends face; see it distinctly. Now talk to your friend about some subject of mutual interest, something different than what you talked about that last time. See your friends expression change; watch your friend smile. Then tell your friend something exciting, and your friends eyes light up with the spirit of fun or excitement just as if you were standing in from of your friend right now.

This short exercise shows you how creative your visualization abilities already are. For most people the obstacle they face is maintaining focus. While they are visualizing, they become fidgety and distracted. They are not accustomed to sitting for even a few minutes without their mind interjecting something that they "should be doing instead". For those who have never used creative visualization, the pictures, sounds and all other senses may not be clear initially, however, with practice more clearness and accuracy can be achieved.

Teaching yourself creative visualization

If you have never consciously taken the time to practice creative visualization, you can teach yourself by doing the following three steps in the order presented. Each step of this technique takes you farther away from your reactive knee-jerk actions and closer to your ability to find a release for your stress. The more you feel you have mastered each step before proceeding to the next, the more you will notice how much easier the following step is for you. You will gain control over your habit to fidget and you will find the interrupting thoughts in your mind become less and quieter. After mastering this technique you will be able to enter a state of creative visualization with very little effort by using the 6 simple steps outlined at the end of this chapter.

Step 1:

(a) Select a room where you can be alone and undisturbed; sit up in a chair (do not lie down), and comfortable. It is important to keep your posture open and comfortable, to support your breathing.

(b) Close your eyes and breathe easy deep, comfortable breaths.

(c) Inhale deeply; and as you exhale, let your body relax; let go, let your muscles take their normal condition with your proper posture. This will remove all pressure from your nerves, and eliminate that tension which so frequently produces physical exhaustion.

(d) Staying awake and aware, let your thoughts roam where they will. If you fall asleep during this exercise, it is an indication that you need more rest. It is important that you stay awake and aware.

(e) Be perfectly still for from five minutes to fifteen minutes. The longer you can sit perfectly still, the better.

(f) Continue to practice this for three or four days or for a week until you can sit perfectly still for a minimum of

15 minutes. Sitting perfectly still means no movement, no re-adjustment, scratching, fidgeting, or blinking. It is important to remember to breathe, so the movement of your chest and your diaphragm expanding is movement you will allow. Breathing is essential ☺

When you have mastered sitting perfectly still and relaxed, awake and aware, for 15 minutes, you a ready to proceed to step 2:

Step 2:
This time you will begin to control your thoughts. If possible always take the same room, the same chair, and the same position as you did for the previous step.

(a) Sit still, relaxed, awake and aware, as before, however, this time STOP all thought. This first part of this step is valuable, because it is a very practical demonstration of the great number of thoughts which are constantly trying to gain access to your mental world. In order to control your thoughts when you are visualizing, you must make space by clearing out the thoughts that interfere. This step is to help you control all thoughts of stress, worry and fear, and will enable you to entertain only the kind of positive creative thoughts in your visualization. For most people this is very difficult. The first time they do this they find themselves thinking "STOP thinking!"; "Why am I thinking"; "Why is that on my mind?"; "Can I do this?" and myriad of other thoughts.

"Little by little, through patience
and repeated effort, the mind will become stilled in the Self."
~ Bhagavad-Gita ~

It is a fact that no two things or thoughts, can occupy the exact same space at the exact same time. Try it. One will either be on top or beside; before or after the other. If you attempt to force two things into the same exact space, they may end up merging into one. So, again, only one is occupying the space.

After you have done part (a) of this step and experienced the effort required to control your thoughts, you can use the following key to assist you in clearing your mind of all thoughts. By clearing your mind of all thoughts you can then begin choose which ones you desire to entertain when you visualize.

(b) Sit perfectly still, relaxed, awake and aware, as you have mastered in Step One, however, this time when you close your eyes, visualize a movie screen in your mind. See this screen through your eyes, not watching yourself looking at it. See this screen and all the space around it, the color solid Black.

(c) Once you are able to see only Black, then see a large white dot appear in the middle of the blackness.

(d) Focus on the white dot. Again, STOP all thought. Anytime a thought comes into your mind, go back to your focus on the white dot. Initially, you will find you are not able to do this for more that a few moments at a time.

Continue practicing this step until you are able to master control over your thoughts. When you have accomplished this, proceed to step 3.

Step 3:

In this step you will be doing two things: you will be visualizing and listening.

Every part of this third step should be practiced with ease. When you have mastered the two preceding steps, this step will be easy and powerful.

(a) Sit perfectly still, relaxed, awake and aware, as you have mastered.

(b) Close your eyes, visualize yourself looking at the movie screen in your mind with the big white dot in the middle of the blackness.

(c) See everything in full color and action through your own eyes. See the positive result you desire.

(d) Feel all the feeling associated with this image. If what you are visualizing has sounds or tastes, you need to sense those sounds and tastes as well. Project all of these images on the white dot on movie screen in your mind. This is creative visualization.

(e) When you can see images clearly on the white dot, begin places images that make you feel at peace. See yourself with confidence, in control of the situation and feeling good about yourself and your capabilities. See yourself in a garden with no worries, or replay in full detail a pleasant memory of a previous experience. Watch the images like a movie and hear all the sounds; feel the temperature and textures; taste the flavors; smell the fragrances and enjoy the experiences you are living in your creative mind.

"Make the image clear and clean-cut,
hold it firmly in the mind and you will
gradually and constantly bring the thing nearer to you."
~Charles Haanel ~

So instead of filling your mind with scary images of stressful events, either real or imagined, replace these images with a creative visualization of relaxing or positive motivating images.

QT 6 Simple Steps

Once you have mastered this technique you will be able to enter into a creative visualization state by preparing your senses with these 6 simple steps:

1. Remember a happy experience – let yourself completely feel the happiness you felt at that time.
2. Remember your favorite fragrance or aroma. Sense yourself being able to smell that now and add that to your feeling of happiness.
3. Bring into your mind, your favorite sound. Sense yourself hearing that sound now, and then add that sound to your sense of your favorite smell and your feeling of happiness. You are creating a symphony of your sensory abilities.
4. Add your memory of your favorite touch sensation to your sensory collection.
5. And season your sensory symphony with your memory of your favorite taste, to the extent that your mouth may actually begin to salivate.
6. Now begin to visualize through your eyes, the scene that will give you a release from your stress. This positive, uplifting visual that your body and mind will be able to connect to and include your sensory symphony. Enjoy your experience.

The more you practice creative visualization the easier it will become. Most people make sure they eat food at least three times every day. They are conditioned to eat breakfast in the morning, lunch at mid day, and dinner at the end of the day and yet neglect to feed and re-condition their mind with nourishing thoughts and visions.

What if 15 minutes a day could actually make a difference in your stress level and living your life in greater peace and confidence?

Would it be worth the effort? Would it be worth changing your habits and exchanging old habits for new ones?

Doing this daily can be as easy and nourishing as your regular daily meals.

CHANGE IN PERCEPTION

*"We cannot solve the problems that we have created
with the same thinking that created them."*
~ Albert Einstein ~

Solving your problems can be stressful or it can be fun, depending on your perspective.

Problems are also the first step in a new invention. Dr. Scholl's foot medications would not be around if people had not had problems with corns, calluses and other ailments. We wouldn't have automobiles today if people had not had problems getting from place to place quickly. Every single invention was created because people had problems with something, so problems can really be motivational! Getting information faster from point A to point B, brought us the fax machine and Federal Express; then email and now Twitter.

Problems also help you to meet new friends. If you are recently divorced, you may join a group and meet some wonderful friends that will bring you into a better life than the life you were living previously. If you have a problem getting back and forth to work, you may decide to join a carpool and save money while meeting others.

If traffic is a problem for you then see the chapter on Road Rage for a few stress solutions.

Coming face to face with problems in life, is not exclusive to anyone. You are not alone. Millions of people who have lived through bad times, and each one has the benefits of learning from the problems that arise in their lives. What you initially label as a problem is also an opportunity to learn something new.

> *"It is one of the commonest of mistakes to consider*
> *that the limit of our power of perception*
> *is also the limit of all there is to perceive."*
> ~ C. W. Leadbeater ~

Unless a problem occurs, you do not learn why something happens the way it does. You cannot change your viewpoints and opinions unless you experience what you label as "problems" first hand.

Problems also cause you to become active in helping others. The organization M.A.D.D. (Mothers Against Drunk Drivers) would have never been born if the founder didn't lose her daughter in a car accident caused by a drunk driver. That one death has literally changed all the drunk driving laws throughout the United States and saved millions of lives!

Without problems, we couldn't solve a lot of future turmoil's and save people a lot of money in business. Any company that introduces a new product will hire people to try it out before it is introduced to the market. These people report the problems they find and the company refines it until its right. Without problems developing early in these tests, the company could never improve and fine tune their product to perfection.

Problems and mistakes are also a blessing in disguise. For instance, Post-It® Notes would never have been made possible unless the guy at the factory didn't mess up mixing the glue recipe. Chocolate chip cookies were born from a problem when the chocolate chips didn't melt as they were supposed to in the original recipe.

However, most people have some perceived notion that making a mistake or having a problem is "bad." Instead of looking for ways to solve the problem, they try and live with it, stress over it, attempt to cover it up and conform their life around it.

Almost every problem can be solved. There is a solution to every single problem you can think of although the solution may not always be what you want it to be - but it's a solution just the same. And covering it up is like putting a piece of foil over a piece of spoiled meat and expecting it not to draw maggots. You have to dispose of the entire thing before you are finally rid of the problem. Attack the core of the problem! Dig until you uncover the solution!

So, next time you have a problem that is causing you stress, look at it logically and with enthusiasm. Love the fact that you have problems because they will give you a way to invent new ways of doing something; new ways that will save you time and sometimes new ways to make money. And when you solve problems, you not only gain experience in solving other problems as they occur, but you build respect for yourself.

You also will find that when you look at problems with a positive mind, you will accomplish more, relieve stress and combat fear, which is the worst enemy and destroyer of all!

"Blessed are they who see beautiful things in humble places
where other people see nothing."
~ Camille Pissarro ~

DON'T COMPARE

YOU are awesome, unique and amazing

Every year I receive several email messages, PowerPoint presentations, videos or poems all created and forwarded over and again. Some of these messages are cute, some incite feelings of love and compassion, and one that seems popular tells you to compare yourself to others. Such as: If you have (certain things in your life), that someone else doesn't have .... you should be grateful (that you are not them, have more then them, are doing better off than them, etc).

> *"I had the blues because I had no shoes*
> *until upon the street; I met a man who had no feet."*
> ~ Anonymous ~

Every time I hear this quote, it sounds to me like an expressing judgment of *"I am better than"* against the person with no feet. I get the same feeling when I get those emails that tell me I am more blessed than people with illnesses, imprisonment, lack of food, in countries where they are persecuted, and so on. In a society that judges others for having less than, and that success is measured by how much stuff you have, this feels to me like: *I am better than you because* I have feet (health, food, etc), so I am grateful that I am better than you and I am not you. Yikes!

Many of us have been raised with comparisons, from our grades in school to the family next door. As an adult, is it helpful or hurtful to your stress level to compare yourself to someone else? Some people believe it is an unchangeable natural human physiology, others believe it gives them a competitive edge. Perhaps. A few people shared that when they compare themselves to someone else; it gives them a lot of wiggle room. If they find faults in the other person, then it relives *them* of having to work so hard. It clears them of having to make an effort to change something in their behavior, even if that change might benefit them. But these people also admitted that guilt that comes with this rationalization and this guilt also causes them stress. I also heard that most people who compare themselves to others, always fall short somewhere, and they are more stressed in their attempts to be as good as someone else. The more you compare yourself to others, the more stress you will create in your life every time you see someone who has more...does more... is more (in your opinion) ... than you.

Dr. Robert A. Emmons, A UCDavis psychologist, conducted a 10 week research in the psychology of gratitude. In one of his studies the participants were asked to list what they were grateful for compared to what they weren't happy about in their lives. In another study they were asked to list what they were grateful for where thought they were better off than others.

The results showed that those who expressed gratitude without comparing themselves as "better than or better off than someone else" were significantly happier than those making comparisons between themselves and others. It's difficult to be stressed when you're grateful and feeling happy.

From another study on self esteem: a dangerous silent damage to your feelings of self worth is created and intensified when you compare yourself to being better off or more successful, or more of anything than someone else. By practicing the habit of comparison when you are feeling happy with yourself or your life, you are establishing the foundation for feelings of lack of self worth when you don't measure up to any comparison in the future. The inherent problem with this habit is that then takes considerably more effort to repair your feeling of lack which can contribute to stress levels and difficulty in regaining levels of success in chosen areas of your life.

A person who can see their unique qualities, success and strengths without the need to compare themselves to anyone other than themselves are found to be emotionally stronger, and less prone to stress, when facing difficult decisions and occurrences.

And since we can only hold one emotion at a time, when we are happy we are not stressed.

YOU are awesome, unique and amazing

"What you are accomplishing
may seem like a drop in the ocean.
But if this drop were not in the ocean,
it would be missed."
~ Mother Theresa ~

According to a UCLA psychological research study, self-affirmations can be a very good combat against stress. In another scientific study they also found that when their test participants wrote self affirming values, their self-perceptions were positively increased, their ability to succeed at learning increased and many other long term benefits.

ℚ𝒯 Affirm Yourself

It's important to remind yourself that you a good person, a unique person and a person of value. Action steps you can take to compare yourself to only yourself.

1. Make a list of your unique qualities and abilities

2. Make a list of those projects you have started and completed successfully.

3. Make a list of those times you exceeded your own expectations.

4. Make a list of everything you like about yourself.

NEW WAYS TO JOURNAL

The term "journaling" means to keep a written or recorded record of occurrences, experiences, or observations in your life. Several workshop, books, coaches and therapists speak about the effectiveness of journaling. You don't have to have perfect spelling or grammar and you don't need to be held to any writing restrictions or techniques. Journaling is a personal experience. For some people journaling means to write out every problem, every thought and every event in detail in a journal, and then reread it some time in the future. For others it means to write their dreams and aspirations and then rereading their entries to recapture the feelings.

Your mind is a powerful computer with an almost unlimited hard drive, able to process vast amounts of information and command several actions related to this information all at the same time, whether you are consciously aware of it or not. Journaling can provide huge advantages when you want to clear your mind for creative thinking; to write what is stressing you so you can re-visit what you were thinking, and look at it from a different perspective and to provide a safe space for your emotions. Journaling is simple and inexpensive only requiring something to write with and something to write on. Using a pen or pencil and a journal book or blank sheets of paper are the most common journal practices, however, many people have moved their journaling to their computers. Whichever way you select to get information from your mind onto paper can help you to understand how your thoughts, choices and actions may be contributing to your stress.

I have used several methods of journaling over the years, from therapeutic to creative; however, one tip I learned from a Tibetan monk has been the most helpful in identifying how the label I have attached to an event or circumstance has an effect on my stress response.

We have developed a habit of labeling events and circumstances as good or bad, stressful or exciting, and we react according to the label we have applied. If we have labeled traffic as bad, regardless of whether it is congested or flowing safely with the speed limit, we will react stressfully when we have to drive in any traffic. Various poll results indicate that over 70% of people are stressed at having to speak in front of a live audience. Simply thinking about the possibility renders fear in these same people. Then they add the label that their reaction is bad, or they are bad for this reaction to public speaking. For some of the other 30%, public speaking is an exciting adrenaline rush. They have labeled it as a good event and they label the adrenalin rush as good. For some people, moving to a new home is a difficult stressful event, and for other it is exciting energy.

Some events and circumstances in your life may have been labels as stressful, when if you look at them without the label, they are more manageable than and perhaps not as stressful as you first imagined. If you forgot something at home, and had to return to get it before proceeding to work or an appointment, you may have discovered something else you forgot. One day when I forgot my cell phone and retuned home to get it, I discovered that I had left a candle burning on my meditation altar. I could have labeled forgetting my cell phone as bad, having to take the time to return home as bad and initially leaving the candle burning as bad, and finding the burning candle as good – and that's a lot of bouncing back and force of emotions. Without labels, you are reducing your reactions, and leaving the option for reevaluating the best action or response to the event or circumstance.

Is what you are experiencing really bad? Or good?

Is the event or circumstance really stressful, or are you so accustomed to labeling it as stressful that you react as if it were?

ℚ𝕋 Remove the labels

Keep a running list every day of the events and circumstances that occur, however write them without emotion, opinion or judgment of good or bad. You do not need to write the entire story of the event, just a one line or a few words description.

> **Today**
>
> *Woke 6am*
> *Left for work 8:30am*
> *Slow traffic*
> *Arrived office 9:00am*
> *Met new employee*
> *Learned new software*
> *Lunch with friend Carol*
> *Sushi*
> *Boss yelled about late report*
> *Afternoon all staff meeting*

Some people could write an entire paragraph about the slow traffic, the bad drivers, and the waste of time; have an opinion about the new employee or what Carol was wearing or saying at lunch. Some people hate learning new software and can complain about it at length, whereas other people love challenging themselves with new learning. If the boss yelled, that is a description of his behavior and his opinion. Some people will stress for hours and even days over someone else's behavior. If you were responsible for the report being late, it seems that it would be more beneficial to your ability to finish the report, if you weren't ruminating about the boss's attitude. We cannot change other people; we can make efforts to change our responses to them.

Keep this non-label journal for a week, and observe how your reactions to usual events in your life may change.

Make your acknowledgement list instead.

Every day millions of people start and end their days feeling more frustration than accomplishment. How many times have you exclaimed in expiration, "I've accomplished nothing today" or "today was a complete waste"? We can get so lost in "doing" that we cloud our ability to see what we have actually "done". At the end of the day, we feel stressed. The next day we start where we left off, with that same feeling of stress. This next day may be eventful or it may be filled with unfinished projects, however, most people will remember the unfinished projects and not the accomplishments and end their day with the same high stress and low energy. And each day is a repeat of the same habits and feelings.

Studies show that, the best time for a sales person to make a sale is right after you made one. The best time to create another success in your life is right after you have just experienced one. Why is that? It is because your energy is now focused on success, feeling good about what you just accomplished and you are feeling a **"success high"**. So it would then make sense that the most difficult time to accomplish anything is when you are not feeling confident, feeling like you are not making any accomplishments and feeling successful.

End and start your days with a "success high" **by** using an acknowledgement journal.

> *"The more you focus on and list your accomplishments, the more accomplishments you will recognize."*
> ~ Brenda Stuart ~

On a clean sheet of paper or a page in your journal, write the date, and the heading: ***What I accomplished today***.

Every time you accomplish **anything** from walking the dog, organizing your sock drawer, exercising, to completing a report make a quick note of it on this accomplishment page.

Write it without any label or description. Just a simple and quick note and keep the list going all day.

```
Date: _____

What I accomplished today:
_____
_____
_____
_____
_____
_____
_____
```

If you are using plain paper, keep your daily sheets in a three ring binder and continue adding to sheets to your binder every day. In a short time your binder will grow and at a glance you will be able to see how much you actually have accomplished. If you are using a journal book, put a sticky tab or book mark at the page you are using for you next entries. Watch how your marker travels toward the back of the book as your pages fill up with your accomplishments.

"The daily Accomplishment Journal has been a tremendous support to me in ways I could not have imagined. Some days when it feels like I have accomplished nothing, I just glance at my list which I keep in a 3 ring binder and I can see one entry after another. Sometimes it's just small things, but they all add up to a day of many things well done." ~ Tracy Marine ~

Download a copy of the Daily Accomplishment sheet at: www.stressout-book.com/stress-resources.htm

CHECK YOUR HABITS & PCC's

"Common sense
is a collection of prejudices acquired by age 18."
~ Albert Einstein ~

We all have a number of premature cognitive commitments, often referred to as common sense, opinions, and erroneously as facts, which were created in our childhood. These early beliefs about reality actually shape our perception and subsequent experiences. Where did you get yours? Most of us adopted our opinions from parents, teachers, media, friends and religious leaders.

---

premature cognitive commitments: (definition)
pre·ma·ture, adj. happening, arriving, existing, or performed before the proper, usual, or intended time.
cog·ni·tive ,adj. : having a basis in empirical factual knowledge.
com·mit·ment, n: the state of being bound emotionally or intellectually to a course of action.

In summary – PCC's are boxing (limiting) yourself to a thought or belief prior to obtaining all the information. These premature cognitive commitments become the habits that begin to control us and our reactions to the events and situations in our lives.

These PCC's box you in, and limit
your creative abilities. Many people feel
this boxing in makes them safe; yet this
gives them a false sense of safety and
security. And the false sense of safety
and security can actually be a
unconscious cause of stress. Especially if a change of
perspective and behaviors holds the solutions and the stress
release.

When we make a premature cognitive commitment, we
usually leap to a conclusion before having enough data to
make a truly informed choice. This may make sense as a child
when we relied on adults in our lives to assist us in our
learning.

Once a person makes a premature cognitive commitment,
once they've arrived at their assessment about a person or
situation, they may also close their mind to any future change
in perspective, and they may miss out on important
information. As an adult you have the opportunity and
personal responsibility to re-visit and evaluate your PCC's.

*"Chains of habit are too light to be felt
until they are too heavy to be broken."*
~ Warren Buffett ~

Common PCC's are identified as: Mindless reactions,
prejudice, mindsets, paradigms, one-sidedness, bigotry,
discrimination. PCC's can increase your stress. They can also
interfere with your constructive learning, block your
creativity, promote an attitude and feelings of defeatism,
eliminate personal responsibility, lead to single-minded
explanations, reduce your sense of personal control,
perpetuate separateness and endanger your self-esteem.

When you are in a stressful situation what opinions and
habits are uniquely yours? Do you react to something as being
stressful based on a past opinion shared with you by someone

else or is it based on your personal experience? Do you react to a stressful event "just as you always have", or similar to how your parents or other adults in your life did?

Are you willing to look at yours? Evaluate them and make conscious choices in your life today? Even if that results in making changes?

> *"Accept no one's definition of your life,*
> *but define yourself."*
> ~Harvey S. Firestone ~

`Years ago, I first heard the story about circus elephants told by Zig Ziglar. More recently I've heard it told by Dr. Deepak Chopra in relation to elephants in India. Elephants are trained as a baby by tying an iron chain around one foot and attaching this iron chain to a stake in the ground. This chain and stake is strong enough to hold the baby elephant. Over a period of time the full-grown elephant is conditioned to believe that this same iron chain tied to a small stake in the ground is strong enough to keep it in place. It "could" easily pull the stake out of the ground and walk away. But it doesn't because it's made a commitment, from it's babyhood that it has adopted as continuing truth, without testing it. It believes that the small chain and stake in the ground is still stronger than it is, as a full grown strong beast. One tug on the chain and the release of the stake from the ground would begin the process of breaking the elephants PCC.

For years everyone was told that it was impossible to break a 4 minute mile. In "fact" a person would have a heart attack by simply attempting it. Roger Bannister broke that record and that "fact". Bannister focused mindfully on his training and not the "fact".

At the 2008 Olympics, Michael Phelps broke all records in the water, after numerous people gave him their opinion and stated that it couldn't be done. He had been told as a child that he would never amount to anything. Fortunately he refused to accept that "opinion" as well.

Throughout our development years we hear opinions from multiple sources, which we adopt as truth without any additional information. Sometimes we are told something should always be stressful. When in actuality, it may have been stressful to the person who told us that information, but it is not something that is stressful to us. What is stressful to one person does not necessarily stress another person, nor to the same extent. Some people are stressed at the idea of traveling in an airplane, where another person is excited in a positive way for the same experience. Some people believe that certain a certain race or gender is not as capable as others based on old prejudiced opinions, even though research and reports state how incorrect those stereotypes now are.

As we grow into adulthood, we have the opportunity to revisit our PCC's and with all the currently available new and updated information, and our collective experiences, determine if they are in fact, true today.

Some people remain trapped by their PCC's. If they accepted something as a child, then it could not possibly be any different today; even though our environment, our technology and our opportunities have changed! If we were told as a child that "life is stressful", then we may be looking at *everything* in life as stressful, without seeing that each event or experience may be perceived differently as an adult today than what we knew as a child.

When we operate within those PCC's we made when we were a child, they limit our personal possibilities today. What appears to be rock solid one day can vaporize the next. Life has infinite possibilities all existing at the same time.

Each of us carries certain deeply embedded beliefs about how we should react to the events and circumstances in our life. Rarely do we question them or examine them or consider how they might be influencing us in harmful ways. Our health, energy, happiness, accomplishments, and relationships are greatly affected by our PCC's.

Only when we stop and question our assumptions, can we see how greatly some of these beliefs have restricted our choices, and how they are affecting our behavior and its outcomes far more than we've realized. This does not remove us from responsibility for our actions as an adult. As an adult you can mindfully notice habitual cognitions such as beliefs, assumptions, prejudices and ways of judging situations and people. You can take personal responsibility for your opinions, choices and actions and choose to make positive changes.

> *"Your time is limited; don't waste it living someone else's life. Don't be trapped by dogma; which is living the result of other people's thinking. Don't let the noise of other's opinion drown your own inner voice."*
> ~ Steve Jobs~

Identifying our PCC's is as easy as becoming more curious about our expectations, and especially knee-jerk reactions. Ask yourself where this opinion or assumption came from. Then open your mind to new possible interpretations.

Stop, reflect, be curious – and then choose.

REFLECT ON YOUR VALUES

"A person's got to have a code,
a creed to live by."
~ John Wayne ~

What are your personal values? Love, courage, bravery, honesty, integrity and compassion are examples of values. Many people are also taught that certain behaviors have value and these behaviors also show value to ourselves and others. These behaviors include respect, compassion, kindness, fidelity.

Your personal values are implicitly related to choice - your choice, and they guide your decisions. What you value tells the world who you are and what is important to you.

In general, a persons values evolve from circumstances with the external world, and these can change over time. For many generations, most of us learned our values, sometimes referred to as morals, from parents, teachers and religious leaders. Family, country, generation, experience, historical environment and your perception of all of these, may also have an influence on the values you have adopted. As we participate in life, the influence over our choice of values may have changed. Today television, news opinions and the opinions of others, may have an influence over your choice of values. The premature cognitive commitments you make also effect the choices you make.

For some people, compromising their values is never a consideration. Even if their life depended on it, they would not compromise and behave contrary to their values. Other people change their commitment to a stated value in order to get what they want in the moment or because of an event. Values are broken many times in an attempt to make another person happy or influence another person. People compromise their values everyday in relationships and at work. They attempt to tell themselves that it's necessary.

Anytime we compromise our personal values, for whatever reason, we are damaging our self-image and our self-esteem, as well as comprising our results. Some times this is referred to as "selling out" or "selling your soul". Honesty is one value that most people will say they have and admire, and many of these same people will lie in an attempt to get ahead at work, cheat on their taxes and spread untrue gossip to fit in with the crowd. This loss of self respect causes stress.

In order to be empowered by your values, you must be clear what they are. The more you recognize and honor your personal values, the more your self esteem benefits, your feelings of self value increase and the world sees the best of you. Keeping your values reduces your stress.

Whatever you say you value, you must also be able to explain – to yourself. If you say you value honesty, does that mean everywhere except the paperclips you take from the office, your taxes and the lies you say to telemarketers. Or is your honesty without disclaimers? Another popular value mentioned is integrity. What does that *really* mean **to you**? Is it the same as the dictionary definition, or do you define it differently?

What do your stand for? What is important to you in a mate? What is important to you in profession, your job or career? What is important in your friendships, the values you demand and those you also give?

These values that you will honor – no matter what! Non-compromisable values are those values that you will honor without disclaimers or exceptions.

This can be tricky for some people. They have been compromising their values for so long, that they have forgotten consciously what is deeply valuable to them. Their subconscious knows this, so that when a person compromises one of their values, they feel stress.

Are you living the values that motivate you to feel good about yourself?

The results of a stress study conducted by UCLA psychologists reported that reflecting on your values provides biological and psychological protection from the damaging effects of stress; including lower cortisol levels, the hormone released during stressful events.

QT

Right now, can you write down your 5 highest non-compromisable values?

1.
2.
3.
4
5.

Take a minute to reflect on your values and what they mean to you; why they are important to you.

If you can start with only one non compromisable value - that's a start. If you don't have one, then choose the one you are willing to have and honor, and start there. When you write your list, honor yourself for your commitment to your values and you.

HONOR YOURSELF

Congratulations! You're Stressed!

Sometimes stress comes at you when you least expect it; even with joyous events. Life changing events such as becoming a new parent, purchasing your first home, getting engaged or married, earning a promotion, moving to a new city or state are wonderful, exciting, challenging, and deserving experiences. And at the same time can open the door to your hidden, 'what ifs'. Those, 'what ifs', can appear like huge black clouds hanging over your head, raining down a litany of your doubts, fears, and worries. What if I can't handle this new change? What if my boss doesn't like me? What if I can't handle the mortgage? What if I fail? What if I hate my new position and this new city? What if I've made a mistake? Slowly you begin to hear that silent scream in your mind.

Stress will continue to build if those, 'what ifs' are not addressed and released. There are a variety of different ways to help release your underlying doubts, fears and worries and one fun way is doing a personal ceremony that you can perform for yourself in the comfort of your own home.

A ceremony to honor yourself, and release your doubts will assist you in getting more centered, grounded, and confident with your life changing event. Ceremonies are a step-by-step process, that guide you into a peaceful and loving space so that you can receive all the guidance and healing you need from your Higher Self. Performing your ceremony will allow you to get in touch with and experience the real you of love, peace, and joy. From a place of love, peace, and joy, you can move forward into your new life event with a sense of appreciation, resolve, confidence, and strength.

You can be creative with the ceremony as well. If you have healing tools that you like to work with such as crystals, flower essences, or essential oils feel free to use them. They will enhance the ceremony specifically for you. The tool that I like to use is my Egyptian Healing Rods because they assist me in focusing more quickly in my meditation practice.

Perform your ceremony when you know you have the opportunity to be in quiet space without disruptions for at least 30 minutes. If, this is too much time and causes you additional stress, break the ceremony up into sections. Use the candle lighting section to set the tone and then work on either the releasing meditation or the honoring meditation. When you know your day is going to be too hectic, take just 5 minutes for the honoring meditation to tap in with your Higher Self to receive a meaningful message. Just 5 minutes with your Higher Self will truly help with your day.

If you can, take some time after your ceremony to just be with yourself feeling the warmth and love filling you.

You can perform this ceremony for a few days in a row, prior to your new or any life-changing event to reinforce your inner strength and confidence.

Clearing & Releasing Ceremony

Materials: votive candle, your favorite instrumental music, pen, small sized sheets of paper to write on, an ashtray/bowl so that you can burn paper, lighter or matches, a bell or singing bowl, and your healing tool of choice (optional).

Find a location in your home where you feel safe and nurtured. Make sure you are in a comfortable seated position where you have all the materials within easy reach. It is important that you and your body can get totally relaxed, especially during the meditations. If you prefer to meditate lying down please do so.

Opening

Put your music on and allow the music to center and ground you.

When you are ready create a single sound with the bell or singing bowl to declare the opening of your ceremony.

Candle Lighting Ceremony

The lighting of your candle is symbolic to your own inner light. This is a reminder of the love and light that you truly are.

Light your candle and recite the following Candle Lighting Prayer.

I am light
I am love
I allow my true self to shine forth to lift me above and beyond to new perspectives
I expand my love and light as a beacon to guide me
Amen

Close your eyes and visualize your beacon of light clearing your way in front of you. Your way is clear without obstacles.

When you are ready, open your eyes.

Releasing Meditation

You will now allow your Higher Self to assist you in clearing away your doubts, fears and worries. Take your time and do not rush. When you are ready declare the following:

I dedicate this time to myself,
to release my doubts and fears
with ease and grace.

Relax into a comfortable position, and if you are using a healing tool, hold your healing tool in your hands, close your eyes, and breathe slowly and deeply. Take a few moments to truly relax your body with each inhale and exhale. When you are ready, allow all of your 'what ifs', doubts and fears, to rise to the surface of your mind. When they arise, write them down on a sheet of paper and place them into the ashtray/bowl. Keep the process going, relax, breath, and allow each 'what if' to surface. Stop when you feel you have written down all you are ready to let go.

Releasing Prayer

The act of burning the papers is symbolic to letting go of all that does not serve you. Recite the prayer and burn the papers.

As I light these papers filled with all my doubts and fears, I release them into the nothingness that they came from.

I give my doubts and fears up to my Higher Self, to be released from my mind, and now I allow my mind to be filled with peace, love, and joy.

Amen

You may repeat the prayer as many times as you like, or until the papers burn out completely. When you are ready, you can move to the Honoring Meditation.

Honoring Meditation

This meditation allows you to tap into your Higher Self to receive guidance and wisdom to move forward into your life with confidence.

Get into a very comfortable position and if you are using a healing tool, hold your healing tool in your hands. Breathe slowly and deeply. With each exhale allow your body to relax. Continue until you are completely relaxed.

Visualize your Higher Self's light above and around you, feel the love and warmth. Allow your Higher Self to guide you to a safe and nurturing place in your mind.  Feel your Higher Self's presence with you, comforting you. Be with your Higher Self's presence for a while and when you are ready, ask for a message of guidance from your Higher Self. This message may be a symbol, a word, a sound, but it will be helpful and meaningful only to you.

When you are ready open your eyes, write down your message and recite the following Honoring Prayer. As you recite the prayer, place the message you received in your hands, and place your hands over your heart.

Honoring Prayer

As I received the loving message from my Higher Self, I recognize that I have honored myself by allowing my true essence of love to come forward.

My love shines within me as a sign of my own inner strength, confidence, and resolve.

I am strong and worthy.

I deserve love, I expand my love, and in return I find no obstacles barring my way.

Amen

Closing
Prayer of Gratitude

I thank myself for taking the time to heal.

I thank my Higher Self for the loving meaningful message I received knowing that only you know what is best for me.

I can now move forward with inner strength and confidence knowing that you are there for me at all times.

Amen

If you can, take some time after your ceremony to just be with yourself feeling the warmth and love filling you.

Visualize yourself in this moment so that if you have one of those 'what ifs' return, you can easily recall this experience and not allow stress to over take your life.

Turn off your music and blow out your candle. Then place the message from your High Self in a location that you will see often.

© Nancy Miiller.

You can learn more about Nancy Miiller and her healing tools in the Authors and Resource sections at the end of this book.

PUSH YOUR OWN BUTTONS

Many of us are familiar with the cliché, "Pushing your buttons"; which means that someone is saying or doing things they know will upset you. You can instead use this cliché to remind you to push your own buttons.

Years ago I was going through a divorce, a change in living conditions and a drastic change in my income all at the same time. I was jumpy and feeling stressed. A friend suggested acupuncture. My fear of needles was alleviated as the doctor I chose explained that acupuncture has been practiced for over 2000 years. The body's life force energy is called Qi, pronounced chi. this vital energy flows along specific meridians in the body and nerve endings that also associated with specific internal organs or organ systems. These meridians and the energy flow are accessible through hundreds of acupuncture points. These meridians can become blocked causing the energy to become trapped, causing distress and disease. A doctor of acupuncture can sense or physically feel heat at the meridian points in a patient's body that has become blocked. Stimulating these blocked areas with hair thin needles which have been inserted at specific meridian points can unblock this energy and allow the body's Qi to flow naturally again, which cam relieve stress and enhance the body's resistance to disease.

Even though I had a positive reaction to the acupuncture treatment, I wanted something I could do at home on my own. My doctor discussed a few other modalities with me and prescribed specific acupressure points that were specific for reducing my tension, to increase energy circulation, and other trigger points to relax my body. Since this book is not medical advice and I am not a licensed clinician, I can share my experience and suggest that you talk with a licensed qualified doctor or practitioner of these modalities,

ACUPRESSURE

Acupressure is a technique derived from acupuncture. Rather than needles, pressure is manually applied to the same specific acupuncture points as my acupuncturist uses which stimulate the body's natural self-curative abilities. Acupuncture points can be stimulated in various ways and acupressure professionals may press, or rub a point in a clockwise direction. To keep things simple my doctor suggested that pressing the points is enough and she sent me home with a chart of acupuncture and reflexology points after demonstrating where to put pressure, how intense and for how long. I followed her prescription and found that it was easy to do, and I did get much of the relief she promised.

I was advised to avoid loud music, exercise, eating, or drinking alcohol while I was stimulating my energy points. I would get a better result from my acupressure, if I made this a dedicated time, instead of one more thing to do while watching TV. Although, if I encountered something stressful, I could press one or two particular acupressure points during the stressful event and find relief. After my treatment, I should allow for some quiet time and drink extra water. During it all I needed to remember to breathe. This was my at home solution I can follow.

 There are several books and DVD's on acupuncture, from simple one spot stimulation methods to more complex instructions, covering several acupressure points. In each case, both from my doctor, and my reading research, pressing the correct point related to the

actual *cause* was essential. Although I could press an acupoint indicated for a headache, if I didn't do something about the cause of the headache, the acupoint could only take the pain away for a short time. If my headache was due to poor diet, eye strain on the computer, or excessively loud noises, when the cause of the headache returned, the headache returned. When I injured my knee in a hiking accident, I could use acupressure to relieve the pain and the swelling; however, I also needed to follow the healing regime to let the physical damage heal itself.

REFLEXOLOGY

Reflexology is more than mere foot massage. According to the Reflexology Association, it is a natural healing art based on the principle that there are points in the feet, hands and ears which correspond to every part, gland and organ of the body. Proper application of pressure on these acupoints relieves stress, improves circulation and helps promote the natural function of the related areas of the body.

Areas of blocked energy are usually a little painful to the pressure when rubbed, and an indication of the energy being released is when the pain is no longer evident. You can work with someone who practices only reflexology or you can gain benefit from a massage therapist who adds reflexology to the overall massage.

QT A quick tip from Ellen Whitehurst, *"By giving yourself a gentle foot massage you're giving your body a chance to balance and remove blockages. Gently press and rub the soles of your feet for a few minutes each day to reduce tension and improve the overall health of your entire system."*

QT **EFT - EMOTIONAL FREEDOM TECHNIQUE**

"Being a single mother, barely making ends meet in a little apartment in a bad part of town was not how I imagined my

life when I was a child, but here I was. I got an email from a friend about EFT. She had used it to help her when she was going through new management at her job and for weeks she wasn't sure if she would get fired. She said it was easy to do and it helped her a lot, so I figured I had nothing to lose. I couldn't afford a class or a coach so I checked it out on the internet. It was easy to understand. All I needed to do was tap certain areas on my face and body, repeat certain sentences and I would feel differently. At first I wasn't sure if anything had happened, so I followed the instructions about doing it more than once. I felt differently almost immediately. One thing I learned was that being very specific was most important. I did this a few times a day and in only a few days I felt calmer. When I was calm I worked better at my job and I had more patience for my daughter. I even had the strength to look for a new apartment in a better part of town. I am thankful my friend told me about EFT." ~ Name withheld by request ~

"EFT is one of the techniques I have used for years. Shortly after being introduced to it, I started using it on everything as they suggest. I felt immediate release from some of the tension and stress that used to be an everyday part of my life. It is something I can use almost everywhere when I start to feel upset, and it works right away for me." ~ Tracy Gelfer ~

EFT is a psychological acupuncture, an emotional version of acupuncture, designed and developed by Gary Craig, a Stanford Engineer, from Dr. Roger Callahan's Thought Field Therapy.　Countless people have reported that EFT helps them to release stress and gives them almost instant results.

EFT stimulates some of the same acupuncture and acupressure meridian points but does so by tapping rather than the use of needles or pressure. In each of these modalities there is a strong belief in a connection between your body's life force energy, your emotions, and your health. EFT has become such a popular technique that several coaches and counselors have incorporated into their practice, sometimes renaming it.

EFT has been reported successful in countless cases often working where nothing else will. Once a person learns what EFT Founder, Gary Craig calls the "basic recipe", they can gain benefit without the need of special tools or additional training. The basic recipe is a rhythmic pattern which includes tapping, eye movements, humming, counting, accompanied with personalized statements. These activities are intended to integrate the tapping effect into various regions of the brain.

EFT is usually quite gentle and a person may often achieve substantial relief with no pain. If they are using EFT to address an existing physical pain, they may experience their pain diminish or vanish during their EFT tapping or shortly afterwards.

The EFT basic recipe includes the use of affirmation statements. Beginning with identifying the problems, and then followed by an affirmation of self love and acceptance. Whether you believe the positive affirmations or not, they are essential. It is common to inflict self doubt and blame when faced with a problem or circumstance that is causing stress. The positive affirmations are a part of creating self acceptance and love in spite of the state of the problem.

This is only a brief and limited introduction to EFT. It should not be considered a substitute for training or therapy provided by a professional. By far, the best instruction for this powerful technique is visual instruction. Visit the website for links to online videos and trained EFT practitioners: http://stressout-book.com/stress-resources.htm

MASSAGE

Yes, my doctor prescribed getting a massage. Getting a massage is more than mere pampering. Unfortunately, a popular opinion is that massage is excessive indulgence, when actually massage can be therapeutic and help you with several health conditions including your stress level in your body.

Massage can relieve tension in your muscles, and it can be used for relaxation. University of Miami School of Medicine conducted a study which included massage and its health benefits, and their results found that massage can lower cortisol, the stress hormone, by over 50%. According to a recent survey more than one third of the people who get massages, are getting them for health reasons.

QT Although receiving a massage from a health professional has many benefits, you can also gain benefit from self-massage. The more you connect with your body and the areas you hold tension, the more you see how your body responds to stress and the easier it is to relax the minute you observe your body becoming tense.

Two areas that commonly get tired and tense from stress:

Shoulders –. You can almost see your neck getting shorter and your ears getting closer to your shoulders from the tension. You can see people pulling at the skin of their shoulder as they attempt to relax the muscle. Sometimes this adds more stress. Persistent shoulder, neck pain or headaches you may think are from your tight shoulders can sometimes be an indication of something more serious and consulting your health professional would be wise. A simple way to massage your shoulders can be done with your fingertips. Sitting upright and starting at the base of your neck use your fingertips to press down instead of rubbing. This makes it easier to locate the exact tense spot. Press down a few times then move your hand to another spot in the direction of your shoulders. Pressing each spot at least four times, and then moving to a new spot. When you reach your shoulder, you can start again at the base of your neck for another round. When you have finished with your pressing massage, relax your shoulders with a rolling motion. Bring your shoulders forward, then up to your ears; press them to the back, and then relax your shoulders down.

Hands - Hands become stressed from too much time on a keyboard, holding tools for extended periods of time and constant clenching. Your hand can be massaged by a combination of pressing and stroking moves. Starting at your wrist, use your thumb on the palm side and your other fingers on the top side to press each area of your hand, both sides at once. Move down to each finger and press all the sides as you move the length of your finger. After pressing all the spots, follow with stroking your hand and fingers. This can easily be accomplished by applying hand lotion and taking extra time to massage it all in.

A quick tip from Ellen Whitehurst in the Reflexology paragraph recommends for you to take a minute to massage your feet.

If you are being prescribed therapeutic massage by your doctor, a specific type of massage will probably be indicated. Massage can be performed by several types of health care professionals, such as a physical therapist, occupational therapist or an independent massage therapist. If you are seeking massage on your own, take time to discuss the various versions and methods of massage with your massage practitioner. In either case discuss what will be occurring with your massage practitioner so you have enough understanding so you can relax and get the full benefits of your massage.

There are many types of massage. Common types of massages include:

Swedish Massage: A massage practitioner manipulates your muscles, skin and tendons, with their hands and sometimes with massage oils.

Deep Tissue Massage. This type of massage is as the name implies, where the massage practitioner massages deeper into the muscles to release chronically tight muscles, limited range of motion, or to work with an injury. Rolfing and Hellerwork are two types of deep tissue massage that also add a spiritual mind-body connection component to the massage. With deep tissue massage, there may sometimes be pain in the muscle area that was massaged for a few days after the massage.

Shiatsu Massage. Another common type of massage where instead of simply rubbing soft tissue, the acupuncture meridians are pressed and held in a specific sequence and flow.

Thai Massage or Bodywork. This is more of an interactive massage. Your body is not only receiving massage to your soft tissue, acupuncture meridians are being pressed, plus your body is being stretched gently into certain yoga type poses. Thai massage should only be selected when you know that your body is healthy enough for this type of stretching and your massage is being given by a qualified Thai massage practitioner.

Reflexology and Acupressure. A competent massage practitioner can not only relax your muscles, but they can provide additional benefit to your massage when massaging these meridian points as I described above.

Sports Massage. Massage to tired muscles after a strenuous workout or participation in a sports event can help your muscles relax easier, and prevent injury from an overworked muscle being used again. At the finish line of every marathon, you will see massage tables and the runners don't hesitate to find one. Many athletes add sports massage to their training regime to keep their muscles in optimum shape and prevent stress.

Chair Massage. With this type of massage you are seated in a special chair, facing forward with a special rest for your face and supporting the weight of your head. The massage practitioner works primarily your back, neck and shoulder areas. This is a perfect massage during the middle of busy work day to give you a break and relax your muscles before your stress takes them over. I recently discovered a few local healthy food stores offering chair massages to customers, and a large shopping mall offers chair massage in a visible retail location. Since you don't have to make special preparations or get undressed and no oil is used, it makes it easier to take 15-20 minutes for a chair massage, and then you can feel mush more relaxed when you go back to whatever you were doing previously.

A few tips to get the best from any of these professional treatments:

Don't eat for at least two hours before your appointment. If your stomach is still full and you are uncomfortable it will take away from your being able to relax and get the full benefit of your treatment.

Be on time. If you are late to your appointment, you not arrive in a hyper and rushed state, you will lose valuable time you could be enjoying the benefits of your treatment.

Ask Questions. If there is anything you need to know about the doctor or health practitioner or the techniques that will be used, ask before you get started so you can feel more comfortable during your session.

Provide information. If you are allergic to any oils or lotions, let your massage practitioner know in advance.

Quiet or Not. If you prefer music or talking during your treatment instead of silence, communicate this at the beginning. If you change your mind during your session, tell your doctor or health practitioner of your new preference.

Be comfortable. Some of these modalities require that you wear loose clothing, so the acupoints can be reached. Although most massage treatments are given to your bare skin, if you prefer to leave a certain amount of clothing on, rather than being naked, only remove what is comfortable for you.

Trust is very important in working with any medical or health practitioner. **You are in control.** If at anytime you feel unsafe, or uncomfortable, you have the right to ask the doctor or health practitioner to stop or to end the session.

Breathe. Relaxed and full abdominal breathing will help facilitate your relaxation. The more relaxed you feel, the more benefits you will receive from your massage.

After your treatment. Take a few minutes of quiet time to prepare yourself to get up and back to your activities. Tell your doctor or health practitioner if you have any discomfort or if you feel weak or dizzy. It may be from the treatment and your relaxation, or it could be a sign of something more serious. Don't drive until you feel you are in full control of your abilities.

Hydrate. Drink extra water after your treatment to keep yourself hydrated.

These modalities are safe and have very few side effects when performed properly. If you have any health issues or injuries it is advisable to check with your health professional before starting any new treatments. For some people, acupressure, reflexology and EFT at home techniques are good, but not enough. In that case working with a qualified a practitioner in that modality would be advised.

If you're considering a new doctor or health professional, choose wisely and do the same things you would do if you were choosing any doctor, by asking people you trust for a referral. Each state and country has their specific regulations regarding licensing and certification for health professionals. Your medical doctor may be able to recommend an acupuncture practitioner or a counselor or massage therapist for you to consider. Many states have regulations and licensing requirements, so check the practitioner's credentials. Some medical insurance companies cover acupuncture therapy, therapeutic massage and counseling.

CHECK YOUR SMILE

Some people overlook how important healthy teeth can be when dealing with stress. Proper dental hygiene is essential which includes daily brushing and flossing

We all know how painful a toothache can be, but it can also add to your stress level.

Even without pain you can have an underlying infection and not know it. An infection can cause you occasional pain, tiredness, headaches, problems with your eyes and potentially serious problems with your heart. Dental insurance has historically been  more expensive than medical insurance. Countless people are without dental coverage and this prevents many of them from visiting the dentist on a regular basis.

If your finances are limited there may be alternatives that can help you to stay on track with any dental work you need:

* ❖ If you have a regular dentist, ask if you can qualify for a payment plan. Some dentists have partnered with lending companies that provide financing for dental work.
* ❖ Some dentists offer their patients the opportunity to make payments with each step of the dental work being performed.

❖ Check with the dental schools in your area. These dental students need patients to prove their skills with. (note how I did not say "practice on"). Dental school fees are usually drastically less than retail dentists, and, their quality of work can be just as good. Dental students are constantly supervised and they may also be using techniques that are more progressive.

According to the American Dental Association clenching your jaw or grinding your teeth is a common stress behavior. Most people aren't aware they are dong this, because they may be doing it in their sleep. If these become habits, they can cause serous and sometimes long term damage to your mouth.

If you clench or grind your teeth, called bruxing, whether you are awake or asleep, you are damaging your teeth and potentially your jaw. You can be unconsciously clenching your jaw when you are stressed and causing yourself jaw pain, tooth pain and headaches. People who grind their teeth in their sleep can wake up with mouth pain, pain on the top of heir head and jaw pain, as well as waking tired from too much activity while they were sleeping.

1. Check with your dentist to make sure your bite, teeth alignment, is correct.
2. During your dental exam make sure you haven't caused any chipped teeth or loosened any dental work.
3. Your dentist may suggest a night guard, and can prescribe and custom fit it one for you. Some dentists suggest you purchase one at a local pharmacy for a lesser cost. These over the counter dental protectors can be adjusted to fit your mouth by following the easy instructions. This usually requires you to place the moldable night guard in hot water first to soften it, then placing it in your mouth and biting down. When fitted correctly this device will conform to your teeth and fit securely in your mouth as you sleep. If you have

any concerns or problems with a night guard, consult with your dentist.

4. Use meditation, breathing and relaxation techniques to relieve stress so you re-learn a more positive behavior rather then bruxing when you are awake.

Smiling is a positive behavior. Even when you don't feel happy, your mood can change if you start smiling. Smiling often can have a positive effect on how you respond to the events in your day. Show your healthy smile as often as possible and enjoy the benefits.

QT   Smile **BIG**

It takes less than a minute to practice this easy exercise:

Regardless of how you are feeling right now, take in a deep purposeful breathe and exhale slowly.

As you exhale - smile.

* Now smile **BIGGER!**
* See how **BIG** you can smile.
* Sense how big your smile is.
* Keep smiling as you open your eyes and continue what you were doing. Most people feel an immediate shift as their stress reaction decreases,

If you have a mirror, you can do this exercise by keeping your eyes open and watch your smile in the mirror. Look into your eyes as you smile and smile BIGGER, and FEEL your smile.

For most people, this quickie exercise changes their mood instantly to feeling better, regardless of how they felt in the beginning.

"This was an interesting exercise. When I looked into the mirror, I saw that smiling made my face look thinner. This is the best non-diet I have ever tried. " ~ Cathi Polenetic ~

BOOST YOUR ENDORPHINS

"A person without a sense of humor is like a wagon without springs. It's jolted by every pebble on the road."
~ Henry Ward Beecher ~

Laughter is the best medicine

My grandfather was one of the most positive influences in my life as a small child. He believed that Laughter is always the best medicine. He was diagnosed with cancer and heart disease so spent his last few weeks in a small bedroom with an oxygen tank. Next to his bed on the floor, a stack as tall as me was issues of Readers Digest magazine. I spent every afternoon and weekend sitting on the floor next to that stack of magazines reading to my Grandfather from its pages of Laughter is the Best Medicine, Life in the United States, and all the other amusing anecdotes. We would laugh together and he told me how much better he was able to breathe after exercising his lungs with laughter. He passed on before my eleventh birthday, and yet after all these years, every time I see a copy of Readers Digest, I remember that feeling of love and laughter and I am drawn to the jokes to exercise my lungs.

Norman Cousins is renowned for the incredible healing power of laughter in his life which he wrote about in his book Anatomy of an Illness. He discovered that when he laughed boisterously at the comedy films that he had selected, he was able to stimulate chemicals in his body that alleviated his physical pain and stimulated healing.

Science News reported recently that employees reported higher job satisfaction when they work for someone who used humor effectively and appropriately.

Many years ago, people were institutionalized for too much laughter. Dr. Hunter "Patch" Adams believes that silliness is a virtue. He is the founder of the Gesundheit Clinic; a clinic which deals with their patients with humor and play, which they see as essential to physical and emotional health healing.

Laughter can make a bleak situation appear more tolerable and clear the energy for creative thinking. Many people have found that laughter is an effective way to deal with their stress. It doesn't mean that the situation itself is funny, or not to be taken seriously.

"Through humor, you can soften some of the worst blows that life delivers. And once you find laughter, no matter how painful your situation might be, you can survive it."
~ Bill Cosby ~

How much better do you feel about anything in your life, after you have had a great belly laugh? (Except my friend who just had tummy surgery, but she'll make up for it soon).

California researchers at Loma Linda University report that laughter reduces stress hormones and boosts your mood with endorphins. During one Ellen DeGeneres comedy monologue she talked about being happy and staying positive, and how happiness opens the door for endorphins. Not being a scientist, she described endorphins as tiny little magical elves that swim through your blood steam, and they tell funny jokes to each other. That cute image alone creates a chuckle.

The scientific explanation is that endorphins are endogenous opioid polypeptide compounds found mainly in the brain and distributed throughout the nervous system.

Endorphins reduce the sensation of pain and affect your emotions. I still prefer the image of little magical elves.

I'm very picky about what I consider funny. I love jokes, parodies, skits and sitcoms which are clever enough in words and actions to surprise me to laughter without having to resort to any racial, gender, political or personal attacks or putdowns.

Television can be a source of good clean comedy, when you watch for it. One of my all time favorite funny skits was seen on the Carol Burnett variety show in the 1960's. Yes, I'm aging myself as I let you know that I saw this when it was first telecast. Now you can watch a video of this performance on the internet. In this Gone with the Wind parody ("Went with the Wind") a broke Scarlett O'Hara (Carol Burnett) tears the curtains off Tara's windows to create a dress, as you may remember Scarlett did in the book and epic film. However, instead of emerging in the iconic green velvet grown, she descends the stairs wearing the curtains intact — complete with a curtain rod thrown over her shoulders doubling as shoulder pads, and the tassel from the tie back as a hat. Boisterous laughter broke out through throughout the studio, and it was a challenge for everyone including Carol to stay in character. Carol Burnett reported that even the crew and her fellow actors did not have a clue about her and Bob Mackie's plan until the second she appeared at the top of the stairs. One of the longest laughs in TV history was created because it was not what we expected, it was better.

Good strong belly laughing is also a full body workout – your face, tummy, arms, legs and back muscles are all get involved. Your diaphragm, lungs and heart all get a workout at the same time. Maryland School of Medicine in Baltimore reports that there's a connection between your blood vessels' ability to expand and laughter, which can lower your risk of heart attack and stroke.

ℚ𝒯 **Share the Joy**

In 2006, researchers at Loma Linda University, reported that just the anticipation of the "mirthful laughter" involved in watching your favorite funny movie boosts endorphins 27 percent. So think about a good joke you want to share or a funny movie you are going to watch and have an endorphin rush twice – in the anticipation and in the doing. Someone laughing will trigger other people to laugh, so it really is contagious. Share your joy

> *"One can never speak enough of the virtues,*
> *the dangers, the power of shared laughter."*
> ~ Francoise Sagan ~

So laughing is not only a free fun experience, science now supports this easy solution to your stress. Laughing can reduce your stress hormones, release your feel good endorphins, give your body a workout and keep your heart healthy. That's better than any drug your doctor could prescribe.

.

STOP! TAKE HEED, TAKE A BREAK

I'm hearing more and more every day about executives and busy professionals who are increasing their doses of anti-depressants and making very poor lifestyle choices that are only increasing their stress levels. It's a vicious circle. More stress; more depression. More depression; more anti-depressants. More anti-depressants; more lethargy. More lethargy; less exercise. Less exercise; more depression...and so on and so on.

Here are 7 simple tips for taking control of your health and your life — even if corporate America is your 'second' home:

❖ Tip #1: Start with giving yourself enough time in the morning to read a self-development book or listen to a motivational CD. If it's a full hour's program, just listen to it for 15 minutes — just enough time to get you into a positive flow for the day ahead. If it's a lengthy book, read only one chapter. But, really think about how you will apply whatever 'nuggets' you uncovered into your current day and its challenges.

❖ Tip #2: Spend the next 15 minutes in your early morning with a vigorous walk; ride a stationary bike or march in place rapidly to music. This will get your heart going and kick up your metabolism, which also reduces stress and increases the endorphins in the brain. Increasing endorphins in the brain will lower the potential for the onset of depression.

❖ Tip #3: Give your body a break. Eat a high protein/low fat breakfast and drink a glass of orange juice. Better yet, eat an orange. Never underestimate the benefits of a good breakfast. This alone will also kick up your metabolism.

❖ Tip #4: Always take a lunch break — no matter how much work you think you have. Do NOT bring your lunch back to your desk. LEAVE your desk and eat in the lunchroom or cafeteria or go to a restaurant. Stay away from cheeseburgers and fries and hot roast beef sandwiches. Eat salads and fruit for lunch or have a tuna sandwich on multi-grain bread. Don't waste your calories on the white demon (white bread).

❖ Tip #5: Remind yourself to drink water throughout the day equal to 1/2 your body weight in ounces. This is not an option. Lay off of the soda, diet sodas, iced teas, and coffees. Did you know that the acidic environments caused by teas and coffees inhibit weight loss and optimal weight maintenance? And the sugars and sodium levels of soft drinks, especially "diet" soft drinks, can also inhibit weight loss and cause many other health problems from cancers to high blood pressure to inflammation.

❖ Tip #6: Breathe deeply several times in a row several times during the course of your day. This is one of the best ways to detoxify our bodies and also stabilizes blood pressure and provides a calming effect.

❖ Tip #7: Take a break for YOURSELF. Remember that if you don't take care of "you" you will not be able to take care of anybody else; nor will you be able to meet your responsibilities at the office. Listen to your body and if you need to take a 5 minute break and walk away from your desk to clear your head then by all means walk away. Trust me; it will all be there when you get back

©Debra Costanzo

Visit the Authors and Resources sections at the end of this book to learn more about Debra Costanzo and 3 in 1 Fitness.

AROMATHERAPY

Although Aromatherapy has been around for over 5,000 years, many people are still unaware of its influence and healing abilities in their life. The art and science of Aromatherapy is utilizing naturally extracted aromatic essences from plants and using these to balance, harmonize and promote the health of body, mind and spirit. Aromatherapy can include healing oils, powders or actual flowers and plants. They can be used in various ways as well. When using the oils that are properly administered, they seem to produce no harmful side effects unless someone is allergic. Essential oils are either burned in a burners or infusers or a diluted solution is used on your skin for absorption. Powders, flowers and plants are inhaled and absorbed. According to a few aromatherapists, using a few drops of natural Aspen Flower Essence in a diffuser, will calm and clear the mind of worry and fear. Scientific studies have also reported that stress can be affected by fragrances.

ℚ𝒯 Use Your Nose

If you don't have the essential oils or powders, you can still use your nose. Let the aroma be your therapy.

For many people the phrase "stop and smell the roses" is a simple platitude, yet the fragrance of a rose can actually have a calming effect, as can many other flower fragrances.

According to researchers in Britain, newly mowed grass can help people relax and make them cheerful.

Your body reacts to fragrance and smells. Think about your personal responses to smell. When you walk into your home and smell your favorite meal being prepared, you have a good emotional reaction. Your mouth salivates, your heart rate increases and you have a good feeling of anticipation. We all know how we react when we smell something we perceive as bad or stinky. Our body can actually revolt in reaction if the scent is strong enough. If someone walks by you wearing an excessive amount of perfume or one you don't like, you have a negative emotional reaction. Your throat can feel like its closing, your nose can itch; you might get a headache and feel nauseous.

You can use various soaps, lotions, sprays, potpourri and scented candles for fragrances that will either relax or stimulate you. You can hang sachets in your closet, around a room or just use bath scents in your favorite relaxing fragrance. Choosing the ones that work best for you can be fun.

The Lavender plant is widely recognized as one of the most soothing of scents which is one reason why it is used extensively in sachets, relaxation pillows and bath and body products. You can try growing your own lavender and drying it, too. The fragrance last long after the color of the flower has faded.

Vanilla is often times recommended as a happiness scent. As one of the ingredients in baking, many people have pleasant childhood connections to memories of the smell of vanilla wafting from the kitchen. When putting your house on the market for sale many realtors advise of their clients to place a few drops of vanilla in the oven or heating vents, or light vanilla scented candles, to permeate the house with this scent to elicit those fond memories of home.

Coffee grounds are a pleasant smells to people, even if they aren't avid coffee drinkers. Many people relax with a good cup of coffee so the scent of freshly ground coffee beans can be very relaxing.

Lemon is another one of those scents that brings back memories of hot summer days and cool lemonade with friends and at family picnics. Lemon is used in many cleaning products because it not only cleans, clears and freshens the air, it creates a feeling that you can breath easier and more relaxed.

Other popular relaxing fragrances include Ginger, Chamomile, Sandalwood and Ylang-Ylang.

Your personal favorites could be the smell of clean soap on your grandmother's skin when she hugged you, the smell of hot roasted turkey in the oven at thanksgiving, pine needles in the winter and your spouse's favorite cologne. Animals play a huge part as well. Just like humans, each animal has their own scent. My cat's unique body scent nuzzle was very relaxing to me and just a cuddle and nuzzle with him could change my entire mood.

Your personal experiences play a part in choosing the fragrance that suits you best for relaxing. Oddly enough one person shared that the smell of garden fertilizer was very relaxing and meant happiness to her. The smell reminded her of days as a child that she spent in the garden with her grandmother planting the spring flowers. Although she probably won't burn this fragrance in her house, it is not offensive to her when she shops at the garden center and she gets an extra benefit from the memories it stimulates when she nourishes her outdoor garden every year. Any fragrance that you remember from a time when you felt happy will take you back to that happy feeling again.

CHANGE LOCATION

A visit to the Laundromat gave me the reprise I needed. I was working from home using my computer on a work related project while I waited for various workmen to fix things that were breaking. It felt like a particularly stressful day. My refrigerator shuttered its last so I was waiting for the appliance service to deliver my new refrigerator and recycle my now old one. At the same time the person who had moved in next door had also brought a family (or two) of roaches with them, who thought my kitchen was a nice place to visit, so the exterminators were also on their way. This meant that I had spent my morning, moving food from my refrigerator to several ice chests, and emptying everything from my cupboards to another room in my home.

All the while not getting any work done on my computer and my boss kept calling for my progress report.

When the appliance men arrived and moved my dead refrigerator it became immediately apparent that the refrigerator had been on the fritz for a while. The drop pan was overflowing and had been dripping onto my floor for enough time that my flooring was buckled and water soaked. Just moving the refrigerator sent this water across my kitchen floor and the wave of water headed for my dining room. It took all my good bath towels to soak up the water. Plus as they wheeled out my old unit, I followed behind on my hands and knees pushing towels against the carpet drops to clean up the path of water drops before they soaked in.

Another phone call and now add a flooring specialist to wait for and my new refrigerator is parked in the middle of my dining room because my kitchen is so small, there is no other place to put it.

And my boss needs my progress report.

The exterminators arrive and tell me that the type of product they are using does not require removing everything from my cupboards as their office had instructed me. So they did their work quickly and left me with my stacks of dishes and cans of food in my living room.

The flooring company called and said they made a mistake promising their person would come today; instead he'll be by in two days and gave me a 4 hour window.

Then, the dreaded final straw. As I started to answer an email to my boss, my computer froze. It seemed like nothing was going my way.

Feeling frustrated and overwhelmed I began to stack up my wet towels with my usual laundry and started the sorting to begin the next few hours of laundry. I own a very nice washer and dryer, so I usually multi task and do my laundry while I'm doing something else, like working on my project and giving my boss progress reports. I thought this would be a great way to wait for my computer to reboot. Then I had a flash remembering how many times I'm interrupted to tend to the demands of the washer or dryer, especially now with this many loads I'd be doing laundry for hours. I decided I just couldn't handle the routine this day, so I packed my laundry in my car, a book into my purse and off I went to the local public Laundromat. A sea of machines greeted me with open lids and a bill changer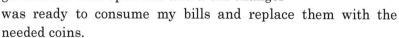 was ready to consume my bills and replace them with the needed coins.

I loaded several machines, fed them their detergent and quarters. As I closed the lids I let out a big sign and a smile. During the 35 minutes wash cycle I began to feel my body relax and my stress leave, as I read my book. The sounds of the washing machines swishing in harmony were music to my ears. No cell phone (I turned it off), no computer, no TV, no repairmen. Watching clothes tumble in the dryer may seem to some like an odd place to feel rejuvenated, but for me that day it was a change of location that I needed.

A few hours later returned home to my soggy kitchen floor and empty cabinets begging for their contents. My computer was rebooted and running properly again. I was able to see how manageable it all was now. My boss had been called into a meeting during my laundry hours, so he couldn't have read my report any sooner than when I now finished it and sent it to him. As I refilled my kitchen cupboards, I discovered items I never use and didn't need, so I was able to prepare a donation to a local thrift shop and have cleaner cupboards now.

So, at the end of the day – it was all ok.

Sometimes a change in location, for a few minutes to a few hours can be all it takes to go from being stressed out to seeing the situation in a new way.

© Melissa Whuel

You can learn more about Melissa Whuel in the Author Section in the back of this book.

FRIENDSHIPS ARE ESSENTIAL

"Friendship is the only cement
that will ever hold the world together"
~ Woodrow Wilson ~

Friendships are important to your health. Researchers have concluded, that not having close friend or confidante is as detrimental to your health as smoking or carrying extra weight! Unfortunately, social activities and fun time with friends is usually one of the first things to hit the back burner when people get stressed.

"All women find strength, comfort and inspiration from their girlfriends," said Melanie Schild, Executive Director of Kappa Delta and the brains behind the creation of the National Women's Friendship Month (September). "In a time of increasing demands, we want to encourage women to take the time to nurture and celebrate these important relationships."

Additionally, a landmark study by UCLA suggests that friendships between women are special. They shape who we are and who we are yet to be. They soothe our tumultuous inner world, fill the emotional gaps in our marriage, and help us remember who we really are. But they may do even more. Scientists now suspect that women have a larger behavioral repertoire than just "fight or flight and that hanging out with girlfriends can actually counteract the kind of stress most of us experience on a daily basis.

According to this study it seems that when the hormone oxytocin is released as part of the stress response in a woman, it buffers the fight or flight response and encourages her gather with other women instead, which releases more oxytocin which further counters stress and produces a calming effect. This calming response does not occur in men because of the high levels of testosterone they produce when they're under stress which seems to reduce the effects of oxytocin. Estrogen seems to enhance oxytocin. (Yay - finally estrogen is a good thing ☻)

"In everyone's life, at some time, our inner fire goes out.
It is then burst into flame by an encounter with another human
being. We should all be thankful for those people
who rekindle the inner spirit. "
~Albert Schweitzer ~

Men and women handle stress differently. A brain scan of a woman when she's stressed shows eight times more blood flow to the emotional part of her brain as compared to a man. A woman's normal reaction will be more emotional, a man's less emotional, however, and neither is having an inappropriate reaction. Generally speaking when a man is flooded by intense emotions, when he's under stress, he can only think in terms of defense and attack while females are more likely to flee (flight) turn to others for help, or attempt to diffuse the situation -'tend and befriend'. During stressful times, a mother is especially likely to show protective responses and connect with others.

Spending time with friends is essential for both men and women to release the stress emotions. Men may get involved in a fix-it project, or yelling at a sports game with the guys for an emotional release. Women who are bothered by a stress can find relief by talking to a empathetic friend. Harvard School of Public Health studies, in Boston, have found that both men and women who have no emotional support are at increased health risks.

- ❖ Find people you can to connect with.
- ❖ Schedule time with friends at least once a week.
- ❖ Keep your schedule

*"A friend to value is the one who comes in
when the whole world has gone out. "*
~ Walter Winchell ~

GRATITUDE BECAUSE...

You have probably heard many people tell you, when you are feeling overly stressed, to just stop and be grateful – for breathing, for health, or something other than what is happening in your life. This chapter invites you dig deeper.

> *"We count our miseries carefully,*
> *and accept our blessings without much thought."*
> ~ Chinese Proverb ~

Throughout my research I have met countless people who can describe in detail something that is stressful for them, why something isn't working or what is going wrong in their life, and yet their gratitude is only a single word or short phrase. I questioned if you are able to explain in detail the reason *why* you have gratitude for something, does it make a difference in the energy behind it? And can that energy shift your stress?

I met people who had similar items on their gratitude list and different responses to my question: *"you are grateful for this because.....?"*

One woman I met with had written "I am thankful for my health" on her gratitude list. When I asked her "You are grateful for your health **because.....**", her answer was *"Well! Because I just am, and I am insulted to be asked why!."* It reminded me of when my parents would tell me do to something and when I asked *why* I heard: " *because I said so."*

In contrast, I met with Nancy who also had written on her list "I am thankful for my health". When I asked *"she was grateful because...."* what she told me was: *"I am thankful I have my health, because that means I can take care of my kids. I brought these beautiful children in the world and they depend on me. When I have my health I can enjoy them and take care of them. And that make me feel such a deep feeling for love and life, that I call that a grateful feeling."*

In order to feel the passion of gratitude Nancy believes that she must be willing to know *why* she feels gratitude. Anything less, to her, is simply not real enough.

I find that every time I do this "gratitude because ..."exercise I find new feelings around each incident I list in gratitude. Several other people shared with me how doing this exercise made a difference in their feelings of gratitude:

"When I was first approached to give my explanation of gratitude, I quickly submitted my long list, the same list I wrote every time. When I took a deeper look at the "because" I found a deeper meaning to my gratitude. Each item on my list had a new brilliance. Looking at my day from this spot of joyous intensity shines a glowing light on everything that follows." ~ Marcie Taylor ~

"I have always professed myself to be a grateful person. After doing this exercise I found I had placed limitations on gratitude and now I find even more things to be grateful for." ~ Michelle Granger ~

"He who knows others is learned; He who knows himself is wise."
~ Lao-tzu, Tao te Ching ~

Another common gratitude exercise instructs you to write *only* three things every night in a Gratitude book before going to sleep. At the end of one stress day, when I could barely think of three things to write, I remembered my conversation with Nancy. I had written "I am grateful this day is over. I read the sentence to myself and added: because... what I first heard in my mind were some of the reasons based on what had been difficult that day. Then as I looked at the journal in my hand I was reminded that this exercise was about gratitude and my thoughts changed.

I read the sentence out loud, "I am grateful this day is over because... and I waited quietly until I could hear reminders of what I had accomplished that day; the mistakes I had corrected, the friends I had spoken with on the phone, how proud I felt to help a client find a solution to a problem she was having.

And while I was feeling proud of myself, what came to mind next surprised me. I consider it a bonus. I saw a flash memory of when I used to be afraid of the ending of the day and the approaching of the night. Nighttime used to be a very fearful time for me. I was feeling proud for helping a client, and then I was feeling proud of myself for not being afraid of the night like I had been for so many years.

That motivated a different feeling. I started to smile and feel genuinely grateful for myself for the changes that I had made in my life. I felt empowered; whereas when I first wrote the Gratitude line, I was feeling stressed and not genuinely grateful at all.

Getting to my "because" helped me during my grieving period after losing my loving companion of 16 years. I had written that I was grateful for the time I had shared with Lancelot. Every time I wrote that sentence or anything similar, I felt overwhelming sadness and tears gushed.

As I wrote every reason why I was grateful and described what I had enjoyed sharing during his life, my sadness was replaced with the memory of the happiness. More feelings of happiness surfaced with each definition I wrote. The sadness of missing him is still there, however, it is being cushioned by many feelings of love and happiness. I'm not grateful that he has died; however, I am very grateful for each and every moment we had shared.

Do this for yourself and see if there is any difference in your feelings.

QT   One Gratitude

❖ Take a clean sheet of paper, or your journal and write something that you are grateful for. Then follow that with: *because*..... and see what you can discover about yourself with your "because".

❖ And observe how your stress energy shifts.

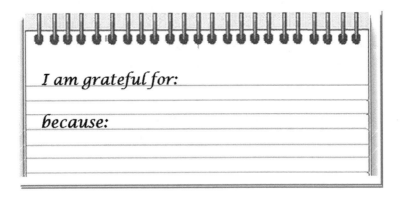

I am grateful for:

because:

> *"The important thing is not to stop questioning.*
> *Curiosity has its own reason for existing.*
> *One cannot help but be in awe*
> *when he contemplates the mysteries of life,*
> *of the marvelous structure of reality.*
> *It is enough if one tries merely to comprehend*
> *a little of this mystery every day.*
> *Never lose a holy curiosity."*
> ~ Albert Einstein ~

ℚT **ONE A DAY**

When was the last time you genuinely thanked the people in your life for simply being in your life, being your friend? This includes family members.

Do this simple exercise to see what a difference you can make in your life by expressing sincere gratitude to people you care about:

🌑 Write a sincere heartfelt thank you note to one person in your life. Just one each day!

🌑 Handwrite your message on an actual physical card or pretty paper.

🌑 Mail this though snail mail instead of e-mail

🌑 The next day, write one more.

🌑 Only write one a day.

One or all of four things will happen.

❖ You will find more people to thank than you first thought.

❖ You may want to do more than one a day. (resist the temptation)

❖ You will discover something new about yourself.

❖ You will feel a shift in your energy, your feelings and sometimes your physical body.

"I LOVE the one-a-day appreciation. I bought a pack of pretty cards and wrote my first note the same day I read this

instruction. I have a go-to friend, the one that is always there for us, and we can count on for anything,. She was my first. A couple of days later she called me because she got my card. She was really touched by what I said in the card. She shared that even though she doesn't look for anything in return for her support of her friends, a surprise appreciation note out of the blue was a great gift. Hearing that made my day too. I plan on keeping this practice" ~ Cameron Grover ~

What difference can you make in your life and someone else's' with a simple sincere note of gratitude?

Start today and find out.

.

Q⫞ HUG FOR YOUR HEALTH

Experts say that hugging is a miracle medicine that can relieve many physical and emotional problems facing people today. Researchers have also found that hugging can help you live longer, protect you against illness, cure depression and stress, strengthen family relationships and even help you to sleep more restfully without pills.

From Dr. Stress Relief

To : YOU

NAME_____ AGE_____
ADDRESS_____ DATE_____

℞ *five hugs every day:*
one at breakfast
one at lunch
one at dinner
one at bedtime.
and one extra somewhere
in your day
Repeat 365 days

(SIGNATURE)

☐ LABEL
REFILL 0 1 2 3 4 5 PRN

A Hug ... The Universal Prescription

No moving parts, no batteries.
No monthly payments and no fees;
Inflation proof, non-taxable,
In fact, it's quite relaxable;

It can't be stolen, won't pollute,
One size fits all, do not dilute.
It uses little energy,
But yields results enormously.

Relieves your tension and your stress,
Invigorate your happiness;
Combats depression, makes you beam,
And elevates your self esteem!

Your circulation it corrects
Without unpleasant side effects
It is, I think, the perfect drug:
May I prescribe, my friend... the hug!

And, of course, fully returnable!
Original author unknown

ACCEPT UNCONDITIONAL LOVE

Animals are known for their unconditional love. We can learn a lot from them

I lost my beloved pet after 16 dedicated years. For some time afterwards, it was difficult to be around any other animals, and then I began to feel the unconditional compassion and love these other animals, my friends' pets, were giving me. These animals didn't care what I was stressed about, what worries I was holding onto; they didn't care how I looked and they didn't care about my career. They just gave unconditional love, helped to heal my heart and lower my stress.

The results from studies indicate that petting a cat can lower blood pressure and stress. Even without petting an animal, listening to a cat purr or seeing a dog's tail wag, can have the same effect. Animals allow us to feel loved and in the present. Animals live moment by moment, not stressing about what they are supposed to do in the future, or hanging onto what they did or did not do in the past. In the Get Moving chapter the importance of walking and taking at least 10,000 steps was emphasized. Taking a dog for a walk usually requires you to go outside and this could help you with your 10,000 steps goal. If you are working on weight control, walking your dog even at a slow 20-minute per mile pace will cause you to burn off about 150 calories each half-hour.

If you can't have pets in your home, you still have opportunities:

1. Volunteer to house/pet sit for a friend when they travel.
2. Volunteer at a no kill shelter, where you can give love and know it's not their last day.
3. Hang around with your friends who have pets. Friends are essential for health, and friends with pets are a double bonus.
4. Visit the dog park and meet people with pets. Ask if you can pet an animal, and when you hear "yes", enjoy sharing that love.

Looking at fun photos and videos of animals can also shift your state from stress to awwwww. A website devoted to sharing the cuteness of animals is appropriately called: http://cuteoverload.com

CONTROL

*"Suffering arises from trying to control what is uncontrollable,
or from neglecting what is within our power."*
~ Epictetus ~

Oh, wouldn't it be great if other people would just change and behave exactly the way we want them to? But they usually won't oblige.

Unless we have complete dominion over someone else's life, we cannot change other people. Yet, so many people spend endless energy in futile attempts to change other people; complaining about what is wrong with these other people and stressing about the behaviors of these other people, even when it doesn't have anything to do with them. Most people have trouble managing their own life, mush less someone else's.

As much as we wish they would change so we don't have to - it all comes back to ourselves. Ultimately, we are responsible for reducing the stress we cause ourselves by attempting to persuade or manipulate other people to change. We can bring it to someone's attention when their behavior is insulting, abusive, unloving or illegal, however, they must be wiling to change, and we cannot change them. The change must come from within.

At a network meeting one day I shared that I eat chocolate every day. It's one of my favorite comfort foods. I also have a chocolate meditation where I savor one piece of chocolate for over 20 minutes. A medical practitioner that day was alarmed by my chocolate confession, and made a persistent effort to make me understand that (in his opinion) my eating chocolate every day was not healthy for me. I don't recall him asking *how much* I ate or what type. He lectured me for a few minutes in the company of several other people that I should be eating almonds as they are healthier. He was persistent in wanting me to promise to eat almonds. I still don't know why it was so important to him that he needed to attempt to change the behavior of someone he had just met and who hadn't asked for advice and wasn't one of his patients. So I promised (partially to get him to stop talking) that I would eat almonds. I'm proud that I keep my promises, so now, I do eat almonds every day - - - - with my chocolate.

Other people can be affected by our behaviors, just as their behavior can have an effect on us. Medical reports indicate that if you are in an abusive situation, you will be negatively affected and your health may suffer. If you are in a loving environment, the effects you feel will be more positive and healthy. If you are displeased with someone's behavior because you have a difference of  opinion, then your reaction to their opinion will affect your stress level. When you attempt to change other person's behaviors to fit your opinions and prejudices, the frustration you experience is creating your own stress.

"God Grant me the serenity
to accept the things I cannot change,
the courage to change the things I can,
and the wisdom to know the difference."
~Serenity Prayer ~

If you have the habit of trying to change a spouse or a friends and the frustration is causing you stress "because they just won't listen" you can take action steps to do something about your stress.

1. Write it down. Write a list of the behaviors, opinions and activities you want them to change.
2. Next to each item on your list, write exactly how you want each of these changed,
3. Next to each item on your list, write all the reasons you need them to change whatever they are doing to whatever it is you want them to do.
4. Looking at your list – why should they change each of these things?

Which answers have you given that are in **their** best interests?

How do you know this for certain?

If you are a parent, this list may be about your children and you with all your experience, could be seeing that their behavior will have a negative impact in their life and their future. Your motives are understandable. If it is a spouse or friend you are attempting to control, how do you know that your choices are better for them and their life? Every day men and women enter into marriages with the thought in mind that they will change their new spouse. They spend years on this mission, until death or divorce ends their misery. Wouldn't it be easier to choose a spouse and friends who we had the most agreeable behaviors, values and beliefs in common with?

5. Did this person ask for your advice or opinion on how they should change? Was there a job posting that you answered that gave you the responsibility to decide

what behaviors, activities and opinions could be kept
and other discarded?

6. How does this person react to your attempting to
change them? In an American Psychological
Association article, it was reported that more than half
of the people trying to change someone else, are doing
so because it is easier than focusing on something in
themselves that needs attention.

I overheard an argument between one of my neighbors.
She was angry with him for smoking because it was bad for his
health, his image and she didn't like the smell. He listened for
a few minutes and then his retort was directed at her for being
over 100 pounds overweight, not exercising and having high
blood pressure that her doctor had told them could be
corrected with better diet and exercise. She knew about her
health condition and the need to change her habits, yet she
was more focused on changing him and his habit. Research
continues to show that the factor that motivates someone to
change does not come from "well meaning" or pushy family or
friends. The motivation comes from within.

7. Now turn the tables. Imagine yourself as this person you
are trying to control and they are the one trying to
change you. How do you feel about that? Do you feel that
your personal rights and free will is being ignored?

If these people demanded you make the changes that you
are demanding on them, would you? If they gave you the same
reasons you are giving them, would you take their reasons and
change? If you say yes then you have discovered the solution –
change yourself to what they want you to be and your stress
over trying to control them is gone.

Each person and each individual situation is unique. We
see others from only one dimension. We don't know all their
experiences and events that have brought them to the

decisions, opinions and behavior choices they make today. Even when those people are our siblings and close family, we don't have personal access to their inner workings to see what input contributed to their choices. When we assume that we know what is best for them and their lives, we are showing them disrespect, not love; we are insulting them, and attempting to take away their individuality and their freedom. No wonder most of us resist.

There is a difference between trying to control friends and family and attempting to control more serious situations and events. If you were the victim of a crime or abuse, you know first hand that you couldn't control or change the other person. Their behavior could have been causing you serious pain or injury, and even though you knew it would be better for you if they changed their behavior, you discovered that you were helpless to make that change happen.

The American Psychological Association reports that when you speak up for yourself in defense against someone attempting to control or harm you, you may feel stress; however, the benefits to your healing and self image are usually healthier. If you witness a crime being committed that you again cannot control, and you ignore it or don't act against it, you may feel guilt along with your stress. Speaking up against something that is illegal, or intentionally hurtful to yourself or others can have its stressful effects, however, not speaking up can have more drastic effects on your stress and your physical and emotional well being. The control over change in these types of situations is changing how you act in response to the behavior or event

"I wanted to change the world. But I have found that the only thing one can be sure of changing is oneself."
~ Aldous Huxley ~

When we argue with another person, attempting to convince them that they are wrong and we are right, we overlook the possibility that maybe both of us can be right; or even, that both of us could be wrong.

The Parable of the Blind Men and the Elephant
by John Godfrey Saxe (1816 – 1887)

It was six men of Indostan
To learning much inclined,
Who went to see the Elephant
Though all of them were blind,
That each by observation
Might satisfy his mind.

The First approached the Elephant
And, happening to fall
Against his broad and sturdy side,
At once began to bawl:
"God bless me, but the Elephant
Is very like a wall!"

The Second, feeling the tusk,
Cried, "Ho! what have we here
So very round and smooth and sharp?
To me 'tis very clear
This wonder of an Elephant
Is very like a spear!"

The Third approached the animal
And, happening to take
The squirming trunk within his hands,
Thus boldly up he spake:
"I see," quoth he, "The Elephant
Is very like a snake!"

The Fourth reached out an eager hand,
And felt about the knee:

"What most the wondrous beast is like
Is very plain," quoth he;
"Tis clear enough the Elephant
Is very like a tree!"

The Fifth, who chanced to touch the ear,

Said, "Even the blindest man
Can tell what this resembles most;
Deny the fact who can:
This marvel of an elephant
Is very like a fan!"

The Sixth no sooner had begun
About the beast to grope
Than, seizing on the swinging tail
That fell within his scope,

"I see," quoth he, "the Elephant
Is very like a rope!"

And so these men of Indostan
Disputed loud and long,
Each in his own opinion
Exceeding stiff and strong.

Though each was partly in the right,
They all were in the wrong!

CONSIDER A DIFFERENT PERSPECTIVE

Perspective: Definition (a mental view; a view creating an opinion)

THE KING AND HIS FRIEND

A King had a close friend who had the habit of remarking "everything happens for good. This is good" about every occurrence in life, no matter what it was. One day the king and his friend were out hunting. The King's friend loaded a gun and handed it to the king, but alas he loaded it wrong and when the king fired it, his thumb was blown off. As usual his friend declared, "Everything happens for good. This is good!"

The King was bleeding and in pain and he was astounded that his friend could be so insensitive. "How can you say this is good? This is obviously not good, this is terrible!" he shouted to his friend. Then he called for his guards to throw his no longer friend into prison.

The King loved to hunt as was very hurt that he had been injured by someone he had trusted as a friend. Hurt both physically and emotionally, but even as his physical injuries healed the king still held onto his anger with his friend. He thought to himself, "just let him think about how jail is happening for good for him!" Later, after his hand healed, the King's decided to go hunting by himself in the woods near his castle. A group of Cannibals were traveling through the woods at the same time and captured the King and took him to their camp. They had woodpile ready and all they needed to do was tie the King to the stake already positioned in the center, and light the fire. When they began to tie him to the stake, they noticed that he was missing a thumb. These Cannibals were very superstitious, and they believed that it would anger their gods and they would become ill if they ever ate anyone who was less than whole. Frightened, they untied the King and chased him away.

The King was stunned but thankful that he was being released, and then he felt guilty. He had been so hateful to his friend who accidentally loaded the gun improperly that caused him to lose his thumb. He hastened to the prison to release his friend. "You were right, he apologized. It was good I lost my thumb, it saved my life" the king told his friend. He went on to apologize to his friend for being so angry and throwing him into prison. That was such a bad thing to do"

"NO! this happened for good", his friend laughed. The King again was confused by his friend's attitude and asked "How could that be that throwing you in prison happened for good my friend? What you did saved my life and I treated you so mean".

"It happened for good" said his friend, "because if I wasn't in prison we would have been hunting together and they would have eaten ME."

##

THE VILLAGE WISE MAN

A village was home to a Wise Man who was revered for his ability to see events in a non-discriminating way.

He owned a beautiful mare which was praised far and wide. One day this beautiful horse disappeared. The people of his village offered sympathy to him for his great misfortune. The Wise Man said simply, "that is one way to look at it."

A few days later the lost mare returned, followed by a beautiful wild stallion. The village congratulated the wise man for his good fortune. He said, " that is one way to look at it."

Some time later, the Wise Man's only son, while riding the stallion, fell off and broke his leg. The village people once again expressed their sympathy at the Wise Man's misfortune. He again said, "that is one way to look at it."

Soon thereafter, war broke out and all the young men of the village except the Wise Man's lame son were drafted and were killed in battle. The village people were amazed as the Wise Man's good luck. His son was the only young man left alive in the village. But the Wise Man kept his same attitude: despite all the turmoil, gains and losses, he gave the same reply, "that is one way to look at it."

##

When we lock our opinions into judging everything the same way, and reacting to events as if it were always going to be stressful, we don't see or don't pay attention to any other possibility. Looking at an event or situation from a different perspective, we can find a way to handle it without being stressed. With fresh eyes, fresh ideas can flourish.

Things aren't always what they appear to be. When things aren't going our way, it helps to step out of our own way and make the effort to see what is happening from a different perspective.

Just like if you look at a room from a different position, you will have a different perspective, a different view of the same room. You have to be willing and receptive to consider that another perspective is an option. Sometimes when you've been staring at a problem for so long it seems impossible to look at it in any other way and you need a coach or counselor to help.

FORGIVENESS

How to Stop Being a Victim of Your Own Stress

I am not talking about average daily stress, I am taking about the insidious stress that we intentionally put upon ourselves each time we recall an event, experience, or person from our past. We hold onto grudges fiercely, then repeat and repeat the stories over and over in our minds. These are the stories that when recalled, bring you right back to that time and place to feel the emotions, the feelings, and even to the very taste in your mouth reinforcing your grudge.

These worn out, overplayed stories carry with them hidden open wounds and hidden hates as we secretly keep them to ourselves, blaming everyone and causing amplified stress to our whole being. Who are we all trying to fool?! The person we are holding a grudge against and blaming in our story is probably sunning their self on the beach in Morocco or enjoying a romantic dinner with their significant other, oblivious to the ranting in our head. They still have no idea that we are angry, they are not participating, and therefore we are the ones creating our own stress.

We all have these stories and some carry on for years. For me, it took five years or more to forgive my ex-husband for cheating on me, and I will tell you, I had so many stories that I could have written 100 books. In each one, I was the starring stressed-out victim.

I tried to forgive so many times, but to no avail. Why does it take so long to forgive, to truly release and let go?

There are many reasons and many times the answers are hard to accept. The list below is the many reasons I could not let go of my stories and you may be able to relate as well.

- ❖ I preferred to be right instead of happy.
- ❖ *Unconsciously*, I secretly loved to blame because it pointed my finger outward instead of inward where the real problem lied and I did not want to take responsibility for my own thoughts.
- ❖ My ego that loves to blame, screamed so loudly that it was all I heard. At the time I was not aware that I was making that choice of my ego.
- ❖ I was fearful to really explore my inner world.
- ❖ I was taught conditional and special forgiveness. I later learned that this type of forgiveness kept me in a continual cycle of blame and stress.

I learned that true forgiveness is a process and a new way to see and heal. I was taught true forgiveness through A Course in Miracles.

In a nutshell, for most of us, we are taught to forgive that when an event happens with another person, when we feel we have been wronged, the other person is made to be the bad person. Typically, we are taught to take the "high road" (I will forgive you, but, I am right, and you are still wrong). We outwardly forgive that person and then forget it all happened, but secretly, in our inner recesses, we view that person burning in hell for all eternity. Then, we feel guilty for wishing that person to burn in hell for all eternity.

The next step for many people, is the bargaining session between yourself and God to alleviate the guilt running rampant though your head. Guilt and fear overtake your whole being because now you are viewing yourself burning in hell for all eternity for wishing this on someone else. And we wonder why we are stressed?

There can be another way out of this cycle, a way to reduce stress, and heal within. You can receive another perspective on these repeated stories, but we do need assistance to guide and teach us.

The Role of Your Higher Self

Let's look at the essence of your ego versus your Higher Self. Your ego lives in the world of fears. The main fear is lack, which translates as: not enough love, not pretty enough, not enough money, not good enough. These are negative and false thoughts that reside in your mind, which then create false images about yourself and others.

In contrast, your Higher Self, your true self in Oneness, is unconditional love, unending peace and expanding joy. Your Higher Self sees this in yourself and others *without exception.* It sees through the false images that your ego shows you. Your Higher Self is the truth about you and everyone; even the person you blame in your cyclical stories.

When you see through the false image of the person that you have blamed to recognizing their Higher Self in Oneness, you have now identified the separation between your ego thoughts and your Higher Self thoughts. Your job is to choose who you want to listen to.

Once you decide to choose your Higher Self then you must listen very intently because your Higher Self does not scream. Your Higher Self will teach you in a gentle and loving voice what you are to learn about yourself with each event that causes you stress. In this learning, you are shown a new perspective of seeing that event. If you choose this new perspective a miracle happens and true forgiveness takes place. Your willingness to learn and heal those wounds eliminates your stress.

Love always conquers fear. Each time you allow your Higher Self in to learn, light and love is shined upon those ego thoughts and slowly heals the separation between your ego and your Higher Self.

The World as a Classroom

"View life as a continuous learning experience."
~ Denis Waitley ~

Accepting your life as a classroom of learning helps you to be open to seeing with your Higher Self's eyes. Relationships whether perceived as good or bad, provide each of us perfect opportunities for healing.

When you are in a relationship, think of the other person as a mirror of yourself. As you see all the good qualities in that person, you are truly seeing a reflection of those qualities that are in you. It is easy to see the good qualities with love and light.

Healing opportunities are presented when you perceive not so good qualities in that person. We all are resistant to accepting that in the mirror. We do not want to own those not so good qualities; especially since they reside in our unconscious. Resistance and defiance can rise up and out, and lead to many arguments, blame, and those vicious repeated wounded stories.

Consider another thought about those not so good qualities. Maybe they were not of this lifetime, maybe it was a couple centuries ago. The other person being the mirror for you is allowing that not so good quality to be seen so that you can see it, release it, and heal it. Now what have you been given? A Gift.

I understand that in the heat of the battle it is not easy to step back and recognize this or even remember to practice true forgiveness. It does not matter when you step back, but it is important that you do. Time does not matter to your Higher Self, what matters is your willingness to perceive the situation differently and practice true forgiveness when you do remember and when you are ready. In my case it was over 5 years later.

True Forgiveness and the Benefits

When you practice true forgiveness, you get in touch with your Higher Self and you are willing to see with its eyes through the false images of your ego. You accept that your Higher Self sees the person you are angry with, as their true essence, unconditional love, unending peace, expanding joy and in Oneness at all times. You accept this about yourself as well. You remember that you are never upset for what you think you are upset about. You recognize the reflection of what is unconsciously in your ego. You agree to allow your Higher Self to shine healing light and remove those thoughts from your mind.

While true forgiveness is simple, it is not easy. It's not easy, because we have been operating with our ego for so long that this change of perspective is uncomfortable and our ego hates it. Our ego loves to blame and does not want to be found out.

The benefits of practicing true forgiveness are endless and lead to inner peace, love and joy. Stress is dramatically reduced and at times eliminated.

For a real example we will look at my repeated story of my ex-husband cheating on me. The whole experience of my marriage falling apart and going through a divorce was extremely traumatic, painful, embarrassing, and of course, I was the perfect wife who was victimized by the whole affair. I won't go into the gory details, but I can assure you it was not a pleasant experience.

For years I replayed numerous stories in my head. Some were all the things I wish I had said, some were all the things I wish I had not said, and some were all the mean things I wish I had done. Some involved my ex husband and some involved the other woman. My mind was swimming day and night. My sleep was disrupted, I lost a lot of weight since I could not eat, and at times I felt depressed and my stress was through the roof.

What was going on here was that I was trapped in my past and I could not get out. My ego was in full gear, and I was blaming my ex husband and the other woman for how my life had turned out. Poor me.

It was years later I learned true forgiveness and began using the process to heal my open wounds, hidden hates and grudges.

My Higher Self revealed to me the illusion of lack I held in my unconscious ego mind, this said to me that I did not deserve love. I released this thought to my Higher Self to shine light on my ego and the false thoughts about myself. I forgave my ex husband and myself. I accepted in both of us that in truth, at our very essence of being, we are only love, peace, and joy. I kept using true forgiveness until I felt peace filling me. Each time I slipped back, I did the process again.

At first and very slowly, my repeated stories became less intense and then they totally slipped away. I still had gut reactions to things associated with my ex husband, like his name, songs we liked, or places we visited so I applied true forgiveness to these as well. Like the stories, these too disappeared into nothingness.

I began experiencing peace, my life blossomed again, my fear of running into him evaporated, happiness filled me and I was not afraid any more.

"To forgive is to set a prisoner free
and discover that the prisoner was you."
~ Lewis B. Smedes ~

I can look back and see that each time I repeated my stories in my mind it was like pouring alcohol on an open wound. My ego in wanting to blame my ex husband kept me distracted so that I would not see the unconscious false image of "not deserving love", that *I* had created about myself.

In practicing true forgiveness with my Higher Self, my open wound was gently healed with love and light. It was healed slowly each time I was willing to see all of us as unconditional love, unending peace and expanding joy. This took time as I made a commitment to myself to be willing to listen to my Higher Self and let go of the false images from my ego.

The Practice of True Forgiveness

To experience the benefits of true forgiveness, make a commitment to yourself to practice anytime you feel stressed. Be willing to allow your Higher Self to lead you in seeing beyond all false images. Below are the explained steps to assist you in practicing true forgiveness.

First, take a step back and get yourself into a calm state. Once you feel you are calm and somewhat relaxed, state to yourself that you have received a false image of the person and/or the situation from your ego. Next, state to yourself that you choose to give up these false images to your Higher Self to heal your ego thoughts. State to yourself in truth you are only love, peace and joy. Finally, you acknowledge yourself that you want to align your thoughts with your Higher Self in peace. Now just let it all go.

Steps in first person
1. I have received a false image of (name) and/or (situation) from my ego, this is not true.
2. I give this false image up to my Higher Self to heal these thoughts in my mind.
3. In truth (name) and I are One in love, peace and joy.
4. I choose to align my thoughts with my Higher Self in peace.

Write steps 1-4 down on index cards and place them in locations that you can remember to use. I had one by my computer at work and one in my meditation room. This helped me until I could memorize the steps.

Begin by taking small steps with practicing. Be aware that you may feel some resistance from your ego at first. That is normal, be kind to yourself. Take is slow, but try it. You may be surprised that the next time something reminds you of that old grudge and you simply don't react. A small smile begins to form with an inner knowing of peace.

Namaste.

© Nancy Miiller

You can learn more about Nancy Miiller and her products and services in the Authors and Resource sections in the back of this book.

SUPPORT WITH COUNSELING & COACHING

*"Struggling souls catch light from other souls who are fully lit
and willing to show it."*
~ Clarissa Pinkola-Estes ~

Would you explore the Amazon jungle, go on safari to Africa or trek the Himalayas without a guide? These mysterious places require knowledge, skill and tools to explore with someone who knows the terrain.

Exploration into the deeper mysteries of your mind and life stress patterns is also more successful with a guide.

Once you have read books, attended seminars, tried a few strategies and still feel stressed or as if you are not making the progress you want fast enough, it may be time to explore finding a guide to help you navigate the unknown territories of your life. That guide is often a counselor or coach.

How Can a Counselor or Coach Help?

*"Relationship is surely the mirror
in which you discover yourself."*
~ Krishnamurti~

Your mind is the resource you consult for problem solving and ideas. Your mind only knows the past. It has cataloged everything that ever happened to you and calculates that same information repeatedly. Therefore, you tend to come up against the same problems and your mind proposes the same solutions. According to Deepak Chopra, "We have 50-60,000 thoughts a day and most are the same thoughts." This is a pattern.

Changing deeply ingrained stressful patterns or concerns in which you feel stuck requires new perspectives, new information and new relationship mirrors through which you can see yourself and the world differently and more clearly.

Also, when you are highly stressed, chances are your mind is not thinking clearly, you may feel confused or find that your emotions are overriding your ability to think.

These are the primary functions of a good counselor or coach, to reflect to you a new view, expand your choices, help you develop new skills and support you in taking new actions into uncharted territory, which can be scary or difficult to take alone.

You can use a counselor or coach:

As a guide to the next level

When you are stressed from feeling stuck at a plateau in your life, business or career, you may want a guide to help you move efficiently and effectively to the next level of growth or performance.

Here again, we do not know what we have not experienced. Moving to another level requires new knowledge and skills. Your guide can teach you what you need to know and support you in taking the necessary steps to get to the next level.

To see yourself in a new way

Your guide can support you in releasing stress through letting go of limiting images and beliefs about how you see yourself and provide a mirror for a new or expanded view of yourself and your possibilities.

There is transformative power in the relationship with another person who is non-judgmental and accepting. In 12-Step recovery programs, this is the value of the 5th Step. Telling another human being who you are and what you have done and being heard and accepted "warts and all" is a powerful healing experience. This experience opens the door to releasing the past and seeing yourself in a new way.

As a model for what is possible

Is your stress related to an unexpressed desire that is yearning to be expressed in you? Are you attracted and inspired by charismatic people, public speakers, leaders in your field? That attraction is stimulating a desire inside of you.

Could you do what they are doing? If this question arises in your heart, you need a counselor or coach to support your spark of inspiration. He or she does this by modeling and teaching you the behavior and skills you need to actualize these possibilities and potentials that are pushing to express through you. The guide may also serve as a mentor, sharing resources and supporting you in taking your first steps successfully.

How do I know which guide is right for me?

Answer the question. "What do I want to be different in my life?

You may not know exactly what is possible, as in "I want to explore my career options" or "I want to know my life purpose." A career coach or life coach would be appropriate to assess your skills and desires, tap into your talents, stimulate creative options and explore roles and markets with you that fit your personality, purpose and passion.

You may want to fix a situation or symptom, as in "I lose my temper often at work or with my kids" or "I feel depressed most of the time." A counselor who works with anger management or depression could be just the ticket here.

Getting Clarity

First, be clear on the arena for which you seek guidance. Is it self-esteem and confidence, relationship struggles, purpose and goals, physical or emotional symptoms (depressed, anxious, over-eating, sleeplessness), career direction, business development, spiritual guidance? The list can be as varied as life itself.

The clearer you can be about the issue and what you want to see as a result, the easier it will be to find a guide who has the background, experience and skills that fit just right for your situation.

When you are clear on what you need or want, the right person frequently shows up. There is an adage: "When the student is ready the teacher appears."

This happened to me. After a year of not grieving the death of my parents, I was finally ready to release the feeling of being in a vacuum or void. I had no direction or goals. I was going through the motions of daily life with no passion or purpose. I didn't know who to live my life for anymore. I knew I needed help, and did not know where to turn.

Within a week of making the decision that I would seek help, my friend told me she was seeing a counselor. As she described her experiences and success, I knew in my heart, this person could help me too. I met with him for an introductory session to see if we were a good fit and began my journey to a new, vital and expanded existence that day. That experience changed my life dramatically for the better. I have continued to use a variety of counselors and coaches to successfully expand my possibilities and shorten my learning curve.

Making Your Choice

Here is a brief acronym that can help you find the right guide for your needs. **I SPOT** a great guide for you!

Intuition

Are you feeling attracted to working with this person? Or, are you feeling wary and uncertain in your body? You must consult your inner physical guidance here. This is a feeling, not a thought. The mind typically resists change and may come up with lots of reasons NOT to engage a change agent, i.e. can't afford it, too busy, it will upset others.... Your mind is not the one to consult about this. Consult your heart or your gut feeling.

Skills

What specific training has the person acquired?

Are they a licensed professional?

What certifications have they acquired?

What unique experiences have they had that built their knowledge and skills?

Sometimes coaches and counselors are coming from a place of knowing from personal experience and success with a particular issue. This can be as valuable and in some cases more valuable than book learning, if it aligns with your desired goal.

Ideally, you want a guide with both training and experience in the arena for which you are seeking help.

Personal Action

What personal development goals and actions is the counselor/coach taking in their own life? Does he/she have a mentor, counselor or coach of his or her own? This is important. You want your guide to be committed to continuously learning and growing too.

Outcomes

Does she/he have testimonials from previous clients reporting their success? Do their clients become more independent, confident and skillful in living because of their interaction with the helper?

Confidentiality will prohibit counselors and coaches from revealing a client's issues or successes by name. Yet, they can share some success stories anonymously with you or a client may have written a testimonial for sharing.

Trust

Does the person instill a sense of trust and safety? Do you feel like you can tell them anything without feeling judged or afraid? Do they speak from their own truth and encourage you to be truthful with yourself?

Although it may take a few sessions to feel a deep sense of trust, you will know early on if you have a basic comfort level with the person. Again, listen to your heart and gut. Don't allow your mind to guilt you into staying with a counselor or coach that feels emotionally unsafe to you.

What can I expect from my counselor or coach?

There are some qualities and conditions you can expect from any qualified counselor or coach. These are non-judgment, a safe environment to share your deepest thoughts and feelings, confidentiality, knowledge, skill to help you explore what is important to you and your life progression, and support for your ongoing ability to make choices and sustain your progress after your time with them is complete.

Helpers are like alpine guides in a chalet at the base of the Alps, ready to assist their next client up the mountain. They are all equipped with maps and tools.

Some are new and have only trekked the lower slopes. Others have climbed a single peak to the top. They are experts on that specialized terrain. And, still others are Sherpas, who have climbed nearly all the highest peaks, know all the pitfalls and risks and can take you anywhere you want to go safely.

If you have general concerns or dissatisfaction in your life, most credentialed counselors or coaches will be helpful to you. If you have a specific issue, you may want a specialist in that arena, who has depth of experience and success with it. If you are looking for a major life change or transformation, you want someone, who continuously engages in his or her own personal growth and knows the deep terrain well. You want a Sherpa.

These are general guidelines. You don't need to over think your choice or let yourself be stuck with the idea of making the wrong choice. If you have explored a few possible options, trust your heart on which one is attracting you the most.

How do I know when it is time to move on?

You may start on the lower slopes of the mountain with a guide who helps you explore and acquire the basic skills to live comfortably with growth and change. This may be all you need for a long time. When you feel confident to sustain the new knowledge and skills on your own, you might want to fly solo.

You might want to move from the lower terrain up a specialty peak. It will be time to find a specialist to help you get to a new level.

When you are a person who has an inner drive to learn all you can about yourself and expand your potential to its fullest, you are exploring with a Sherpa. There will be times when you want to quit. Your mind will create reasons to stop prematurely, especially when a big shift is right around the corner. Be sure to discuss any thoughts about ending the relationship with your counselor or coach along the way. They can help you to determine if you are ready to stop because your growth is complete to that point or if you are about to breakthrough to a new level and being tempted to avoid that shift.

Just know that finding new guides as you grow and change is fine. It does not indicate that your original or current helper is deficient in any way.

At the same time, be aware that sometimes your urge to change guides may be a sign that inner change is right around the corner. Don't leave in haste. Do discuss your decision with your counselor or coach.

Investment

In difficult economic times or when limited finances are part of your stress, it may be hard to justify spending money on coaching or counseling. A financial counselor may be the first guide you need. Often, financial counseling or coaching resources can be found at low cost or for free, as Consumer Credit Counseling for example.

For other stress areas, look upon your counselor or coach's fees as a wise investment in yourself and your life success. Coaches and counselors can shortcut your learning curve by years, thus opening you to greater success and prosperity quickly. Investing in your personal growth is one of the most beneficial investments you can make.

Newer coaches and counselors generally have lower fees, while specialists and Sherpas may require a higher investment.

Some coaches have programs that extend for several weeks or months, which give you the opportunity to reduce the cost of hourly fees by investing in the program.

Summary

As children, we grow up seeing ourselves and defining our life through the mirrors (eyes) of our parents, teachers and other significant relationships. As we grow up, those original images and beliefs become repetitive patterns that can interfere with our growth and progress in an ever changing and evolving world.

When conflict arises between your original image and your need to express yourself more fully in the world, symptoms of stress arise to create the tension and friction needed for change.

Use your own intuition and the questions and guidelines in this chapter as a starting point for finding a counselor or coach who is just the right fit for your needs.

Make a commitment to yourself to see your changes through to your desired outcomes.

"To grow, you must be willing to let your present and future be totally unlike your past. Your history is not your destiny."
~ Alan Cohen ~

A Personal Intention for You

May you attract the perfect guides to help you expand the boundaries of belief in your potential and possibilities on the road toward fulfilling your destiny.

© 2009 Aila Accad, RN, MSN

You can learn more about Aila Accad RN, MSN in the Author and Resource sections at the back of this book.

GET UP AND MOVE

It's nagging time. It seems that whether the topic is weight management or stress release, the number one solution consistently recommended is *exercise*. Several studies prove that all forms of physical activity assist in reducing our stress. Our stress response prepares us to fight or flee and our bodies are primed for action. Unfortunately, since we usually handle our stress while sitting at our desk, standing at the water cooler or behind the wheel stuck in traffic, that fight or flight stress adrenalin stays in our body. When we exercise on a regular basis it helps to release that pent up energy as well as turning down the production of new stress neurochemicals.

Most people are smart enough to know that they should set some time aside to exercise. Moderate to strong exercise 3 times a week for a minimum of 30 minutes can make a significant difference over time, in how your body responds to stress, and how quickly you recover. If you participate in some sports activity, remember you're doing it for your health! While many people naturally have their competitive nature come to the surface when engaging athletics, don't lose sight of the fact you're participating to have fun. Don't get bent out of shape if you don't always win or otherwise play up to par. The whole point is to enjoy yourself and forget your everyday worries.

Nearly every day someone is telling us that exercise is important to our physical and mental health. But seldom do they ever comment on how boring it can be. Especially when you are doing it alone.

> *"The only reason I would take up jogging*
> *is so that I could hear heavy breathing again."*
> ~ Erma Bombeck ~

Years ago I heard Zig Ziglar say, that *"for most people their idea of exercise is to fill the bathtub, pull the plug and fight the current."* Practicing abdominal breathing is the most exercise that some people give to their mid region. And other people consider the movement of their jaw during chewing or talking to be an aerobic exercise. As comical as these sound, there are fun real exercise alternatives.

One excuse most commonly given against exercise is not having enough time. It's been proven that we always find time to do those things that we consider important. It's time to make yourself important to you.

10,000 steps

Over the years, the US Surgeon General's office has issued reports based on extensive research, to educate and provide us with recommendations that can help us to live healthier lives. In 2000 the National Health Interview Survey reported that only *"15% of adults aged 18 years and older engaged in moderate physical activity for at least 30 minutes 5 or more days per week. The adoption and maintenance of regular physical activity represent an important component of any health regime and provide multiple opportunities to improve and maintain health."* The report went on to recommend that moderate physical activity, for example, could be a brisk walk for only 30 minutes per day which equals approximately 10,000 steps. After this report was first released their was a slight interest and change in the number of people who increased their physical activity and just like so many new years resolutions, the interest and participation soon waned.

At one time several companies McDonalds, Del Monte Foods and Tylenol for example, promoted walking health by offering free pedometers. Yet today, even though reports continue to prove that physical activity assists in reducing our stress, researchers are still finding that the majority of the population walks far less than 10,000 steps, some only as little as 2000 steps. And some of the least active people are those with home based businesses. With a thirty-second commute to their home office desk and computer, many of them stay there for the entire day, and *barely total 500 steps a day.*

Q.T You can add healthy steps to your day in a few different ways:

- ❖ Use the stairs instead of the elevator.
- ❖ Walk your dog one extra block.
- ❖ Let someone else have that close to the door parking space and park on the other side of the parking lot instead.
- ❖ Get up from your desk at least once an hour and walk around the office; and if you work from home, add more steps by walking around the block.
- ❖ Find errands that you can walk to instead of driving.
- ❖ Find a walking buddy.
- ❖ Instead of forwarding through the commercials in your recorded television shows do something old fashioned. Mute the sound and get up and walk around, march in place or stretch and breathe. At each commercial break, make this time for your health and take a few more steps.

Don't let the weather always determine if you are going to exercise. Go to a local indoor mall that is temperature controlled and take a brisk walk through the mall courtyard. Leave your credit cards at home so you won't be tempted to stop and shop. Window shop as you walk by.

Prior to publishing this book, I searched for any current free pedometer offers, and was unable to find any; however that should not stop you from getting up and walking. Any new free offers or specials we find for products to assist you in adding 10,000 steps to your day, and making it fun, will be announced in the Stress Out Daily Tips e-zine.

Although physical activity is perfectly safe for most people, not every body is the same. If you have or had serious health conditions it's advisable to consult with your doctor before you take on a new exercise program, or enter into one that will challenge the limits of your body. Don't let your current health be an excuse to keep you from exercise. Ask your doctor or health professional for recommendations that you can follow.

Support a Cause

A great way get exercise, have fun, meet new people and do something for someone else is to participate in a program that benefits a charity. When you make any of these commitments you are more motivated to keep your word.

1. Join the Sierra Club and help clean up trails and plant trees.
2. Volunteer with Habitat for Humanity and wield a hammer.
3. Participate in a sports fundraiser for a charity. You don't have to commit to a marathon, some charities have sports events from one mile walks, 5K 10K, half or full marathons, and other events as well. If you have never considered a marathon, you may think that a person who participates in marathons is a bit crazy. I used to and some of my friends don't hesitate to tell me how crazy I am when I share how good it feels to cross that finish line after 26.2 miles. I never thought I would do a marathon. Now I am hooked. It is exciting to push your healthy limits while helping other people reach their goals.

When you commit to participate in a fundraising sport:
* ❖ You will see the benefits of eating properly as you maintain your workout schedule for the event.
* ❖ Your body will be tired enough to help you sleep.
* ❖ You will prioritize and find ways to master your schedule.
* ❖ The beauty of the landscape along the route is energizing.

And when you cross the finish line:
* ❖ You will find yourself smiling.
* ❖ You will feel great about your accomplishment.

It's difficult to feel stress with these actions and feelings. You will find that some of your old excuses against exercise just seem to disappear.
* ❖ Usually no age limitations. At one charity sports event, the youngest person was under 15 and the oldest was in her 70's.
* ❖ You don't always have to run. Training teams now teach a run/walk technique to use more muscles effectively and for people who aren't professional athletes. At one marathon, I saw people on the road with me who wore prosthesis, and some who were running barefoot.

Whether you are training for one mile for 26.2, it's easier to stay healthy and injury free when you follow a proper training schedule. Accidents can happen, however, the stronger your body is from the training, the better your chances are to finish top of your form, exhausted and feeling good about yourself. Before starting any new or more strenuous exercise program, you may want to talk to your doctor first.

So whether you run, walk or combo – choose a cause, get out and get moving.

On the Stress Out website, we have listed several non profit organizations that have several various athletic events for fundraising, including:

* Arthritis - (5K and Marathon), www.arthritis.org
* American Lung Assn Healthy Air Walk, www.lungusa.org
* American Cancer Society (Relay for Life), www.cancer.org
* Susan G. Komen Foundation, www.komen.org
* American & Canadian Diabetes Assn, http://walk.diabetes.org
* American Heart Assn Heart 5K Walk,www.americanheart.org

Visit the website for an exercise related event in your area: www.stressout-book.com/stress-resources.htm

☙ DANCE

If you tuned into Oprah's 24th Season Kickoff Party you witnessed thousands of people in an audience all dancing together in sync to a very upbeat song. The replay on YouTube has been viewed millions of times, and the comments indicate that people are dancing to this song all over the world because it makes them feel happy.

"I play this song every day, and now when I get up in the morning, what is ringing in my head are the words "Today is gonna be a good, good day..." I find myself dancing around and feeling great, for no real reason other than the music makes me want to dance." ~ Precilla Junart ~

Dancing with the Stars and Can You Dance television shows have stimulated an increase in dance lessons and have given couples one more fun activity to share. More people are discovering the benefits of dancing as exercise, as a positive mood changer, and stress release.

Stress activates a fight or flight response. Since most of us don't flee from our stress, and hopefully don't have to resort to fighting, that energy stays in our body. This unspent energy can cause agitations and reactions long after the event is gone. If the stress event or circumstance is ongoing, the energy is never discharged and it can remain in your nervous system, ready to react to the next event. Even if it isn't a stressful event, you are going into it on edge.

Dancing is one healthy way to move your body to release the energy and have fun at the same time.

You've seen athletes such as sprinters and runners, at the starting line ready for the race. They fidget; some kick their feet and shake their hands. I've witnessed people behind stage ready for a presentation, pacing back and forth. They are feeling the force of their excitement energy and their fidgeting is helping them to release the excess. You can also release some of your pent-up stress energy by shaking your hands and kicking your feet.

So combine the two – make your dancing animated and full of movement. Instead of following a routine which can be stressful for some people trying to remember the steps, just move your arms, in your own style, Get excited, work up a sweat, sing along and dance your stress away.

ℚᴛ STRETCH, BREATHE, LAUGH

When you are stressed you can be stuck in more ways than one. Physically stand up. This exercise will take you through physical movements while standing in one spot, to assist you in moving the energy in your body.

Locate a place where you can stand in the same spot for the duration of this exercise regardless of what is happening around you or in your mind. Stop and take in a very deep breathe. As you are breathing in, be conscious of how full your lungs become. With each inhale breathe make yourself as big as you can. Then on the exhale, relax while still standing in good posture. Breathe in this way at least 3 times.

On the fourth breath, as you inhale, interlace your fingers and raise your arms over your head with the palm of your hands now facing the sky. Reach as high as you can and stretch as much as you can. Keep breathing.

Take in another deep breathe and on the exhale, relax and begin to flow forward from your waist, letting your arms hang freely at your sides. Bend only as far as is comfortable and keep your knees relaxed, not straight legged. This is not an exercise to force you to stretch farther.

In this bent over position, relax and continue to breathe.

Some people, especially if you have extra padding in the mid region, may find it difficult to take in a deep breath in this bent over position. According to a news release, studies conducted at Wake Forest University indicated that stress can add belly fat. And when the researchers took a deeper look at the test subjects, they found that fat was also blocking their arteries, which raises the risk factors for heart disease. So if you are finding it difficult to take in a deep breath in this relaxed bent over position – check your belly and check in with your health professional to help you do something about it.

After a couple of breaths, take in another deep breath and bring yourself back up to your standing position with your arms stretched over your head again.

Do this breathing and bending over **two more times.**

On the third time you will be doing something other than just exhaling.

On this third time, *LAUGH* as you bend forward from your waist. Laugh all the way down as you are exhaling. Laugh as you are bent over and breathing.

From this bent over position, take in your next breathe and bring yourself to your standing position again with your arms stretched towards the sky.

Two more times, exhale and laugh your way down to your bent over position. Laugh while you relax in your bent over position with another breath. Take a deep breath each time you bring yourself back to your standing position with your arms stretched towards the sky.

After you have stretched and bent over laughing three times, stand comfortably with your arms at your sides, and breathe normally a few breathes.

Close your eyes, continue breathing comfortably and fully, and let yourself think of **one** thing you are grateful for. Only one. Even one tiny thing. I will not give you the platitude said by too many people that you *"should be grateful that you are breathing."* If you are having a bad day or you feel like you are overly stressed – that recommendation could seem more like an uncaring platitude. **You choose** what you are grateful for, from the voice deep inside of you. On days when my stress level was high, and it appeared that everything was going wrong in my life, I sometimes had to search for a tiny thing. Some days in the midst of my misery I could only be grateful that I saw the spider before he saw me. That is a beginning. You only need a crack in the door of darkness to begin to see the light.

FLY A KITE

Oh, go fly a kite. This phrase can be used as a command and an intended insult when someone wants you to quit bothering them. So go fly a kit – with your stress. Give your stress to the wind

As a child, building a kite from scratch was fun and it added to a good feeling of accomplishment as we all watched our kites bob and weave in the air. Add to that the wind tousling our hair and clothes, it felt like freedom.

Yes, this solution seems to be more easily done in spring and summer unless you are billowing out enough hot air to set a kit into flight. However, just because the weather outdoors may not be kite weather, you can still use your creative visualization abilities and revisit your memories of when you last flew a kite. Close your eyes and see your hand holding that string, your kite bouncing in the air to the wind and feel all the joy. Feel the wind in your face and breathe it in, relaxed – and smile.

So - go fly a kite!

HYDRATE YOUR BODY & MIND

Water is our body's vital fuel. It's a calorie-free, inexpensive and easily obtained health drink from Mother Nature. Yet few people follow the old fashioned advice to drink enough water every day. Most Americans are chronically dehydrated. Studies have shown that being dehydrated can actually induce stress.

Most people drink when they are thirsty, but the beverage of choice tends to be some other drink besides water. Based on an analysis of all fluid intakes by adults, it is reported to total about two quarts of water a day; and this includes water from foods and from other beverages. It's usually not necessary to actually swallow two quarts of plain water every day, however, people with special health needs, high stress and intense levels of physical exertion are exceptions.

Americans drink eight gallons of bottled water a year, roughly two ounces or a quarter-cup a day, according to the International Bottled Water Association. Californians drink three times the national average of bottled water, downing 24 gallons a year, or nearly a cup a day. Climate and seasons of the year play a role in one's thirst also, and just as we tend to perspire more in the summer months, we also tend to drink more water.

Who should drink water? We all should. When it is hot or humid, upping your water intake is also wise. Boosting intake of plain water makes good sense, many experts concur, because water eases digestion, regulates body temperature, helps control certain fears and reduces stress.

Water also bathes your cells, accounts for about 85% of brain tissue and 60% of your total body weight. Drinking water can ward off constipation and maybe even crankiness. And since it's a natural appetite suppressant, water can help us lose weight and keep it off.

Drinking fluids, particularly water, during exercise reduces cardiovascular stress and improves performance. After a strenuous workout, you have to replace the fluids you have lost. Otherwise, you will suffer chronic dehydration. Drink water before, during and after exercising and remember that water reduces body temperature thus making the whole exercise process safer. Get into the habit by starting with a glass of water with every meal, then work in a cup between meals.

ꝗT Drink More Water

A small change makes a big difference when it comes to water. For today, exchange one optional fluid (i.e.: soda, coffee, alcohol, tea, etc) for one glass of pure water. First thing in the morning before your first cup of coffee, drink a cold glass of water instead.

Aside from drinking water, taking a bath is a calming remedy for stress and anxiety. Bathing is essential to your health and peace of mind.

"This bath will make you feel like a million while washing all issues, worries and concerns down the drain. Take a handful of fresh oregano (unless you're pregnant, then PLEASE find some other way to relax!) and give it a rough chop all the while visualizing a calm, cool and really relaxed you. Now put the oregano in a bowl and add a quarter cup of either almond or jojoba oil.

Then add the juice from three fresh oranges to this mix. Let sit and marinate together for 15 to 20 minutes. Run a bath, add two cups of Epsom or sea salt and then pour in the oregano mix before soaking for just slightly less than a half hour. To increase the relaxing power associated with this bath you should burn a purple or white candle while you bathe while also playing calming and centering music. Wash your cares away and, of course, enjoy! " © Ellen Whitehurst

"There must be quite a few things that a hot bath won't cure,
but I don't know many of them."
~ Sylvia Plath ~

WHAT ARE YOU EATING AND WHAT'S EATING YOU?

Have you heard yourself and others say this before:

"I always eat when I'm upset, stressed, bored..." You pick the emotion or life's circumstance that has caused you to either overeat or eat the wrong things.

Do you turn to the cookies, bread and candy whenever things don't turn out as you'd planned?

With all the stress in your life right now, do you feel that food to be your only solace?

Have you heard yourself saying - "I love food and I don't want to give it up or feel like I need to restrict myself - I need it right now to get me over this stressful period in my life

Why do we eat?
- ❖ Nourishment
- ❖ Pleasure
- ❖ Because we should
- ❖ Because we have to
- ❖ Because we LOVE FOOD
- ❖ Eating brings us comfort

And why do we reach for food when stressed out?

Even though some individuals actually stop eating under stress, many of us tend to eat more, the wrong things and at the wrong time.

Clues to discovering if you are a Stress Eater:
1. **Hunger comes on suddenly.**
   Physical hunger comes on slowly. Hunger from emotional eating often comes on quickly and is usually a reaction to some situation or some person or group of people. It can be either positive or negative. Our emotions take over sending a signal to our salivary glands and then that familiar feeling of being out of control takes over. We want something and we want it now! One alternative may be counting to 60. Or another would be to eat some protein which will actually calm you down right away, versus "using" sugary, starchy or the forbidden foods.
2. **Cravings.**
   Not usually carrot sticks or steamed broccoli. A craving for a specific, usually unhealthy food is often a sign of emotional eating. Often people like the rush they get from satisfying their cravings. That rush is fulfilling emotional hunger not physical hunger. This feeling is quite fleeting and yet we often remember the "release" of tension it often provides us.
3. **Hunger feels urgent.**
   You need a particular food right away and you're willing to walk out of your way, or get in your car late at night, or raid your kid's Halloween candy to get it. This is often a very good sign that an addictive pattern is taking hold of you. Cigarette smokers will often walk through a blizzard to get their "fix" – that

actually happened to me a couple of times when I must admit I was a smoker in my early 20's. You can't live without it – you must have it! Physical hunger, unless you haven't eaten for a very long time, is usually pretty patient and will wait for food. Emotional hunger demands to be satisfied immediately. My mother often says "Hunger is the best cook." When you are genuinely hungry – almost everything tastes good.

4. **Hunger triggered by an upsetting emotion.**

If you find yourself overeating, going for the sweets or salty treats and snacks you might want to backtrack a few hours. Was there a particular upsetting event that triggered the urge? Most out of whack emotional eating occurs right after a stressful, often acute, situation. Perceived hunger connected to an upsetting situation usually an emotional hunger. Physical hunger is not typically triggered by emotions – it's usually determined by length of time between meals or after exerting a lot of energy in a project, an exercise regimen or some super human feat. The mental or physical exertion uses up more energy (calories) therefore requiring additional calories to keep you going.

5. **Unconscious eating.**

All of a sudden you realize you're eating the last spoonful of ice-cream from the carton while busily working away or watching TV. In shock you feel like an out of control glutton, ashamed of yourself. Or you sit at the dinner table and happily polish off a meal suited to 300 lbs Sumo Wrestler. You feel uncomfortable, bloated and swear you'll never eat another meal as long as you live.

The Solutions

1.   Allow yourself time if you going through a
particularly   emotional   time.   This   is   so
important. We've all had times in our lives when life is
really tough. A year ago I experienced an extremely
stressful and sad time in my own personal life - I lost
one of my brothers in a very sudden and tragic
accident. During this time I allowed myself to grieve
and to eat things I wouldn't normally gravitate towards
on a daily basis. I drank wine, ate late and simply
allowed myself to eat what and when I wanted to or
needed to.   There were times when food was the
furthest thing from my mind and other times when I
was ravenous.   We all have these stressful times
whatever the reason so it's really important to allow
yourself to go through it and feel all the feelings. Don't
deny your feelings and say you need to get over it
before you are ready.   You actually may not be
emotionally ready to move on. While going through
tough times or tragedies, and they do happen for all of
us, try as much as you possibly can to commit again to
taking care of yourself by eating well, exercising and
treating yourself like gold. No matter what you are
going through you still have a contribution to make - so
do take care and nurture yourself and allow others
help you, too. You are not an island and there are
many close to you who want to and can help you get
though the challenges. And don't let it drag on. You
owe it to yourself to get back on track as soon as you
can.

2.   Eat regular meals and take a break when eating.
Try not to eat when you are busy doing other things
like reading, watching TV, etc. If you do this your
brain actually doesn't compute that you might have
just had a 3 course meal.   When you are engaged in

other activities you are more likely to keep on eating and eating until it's too late. If you are busy doing other things a major miscommunication takes place between your brain and your stomach well in fact within your whole digestive system. The brain asks "did I just eat?" and consciously you really haven't even though your belly is full. Ignoring signals like this and trying to multi-task while eating only perpetuates the tendency to overeat causing further stress to your digestive system and your psychology. So take your time and eat as slowly as you can. Make a point of being aware of what and how you are eating and do slow down. Doing something as simple as sitting at the dining room table, lighting a candle and pulling out some fine linen – will not only prevent you from overeating but also you will feel less stressed, calmer and you may even feel nurtured and quite special. If the linens and candles are too much – just try sitting at your table instead of in front of the TV.

3.   Eat protein and you'll be less likely to overeat. Most people undergoing   stressful   times usually gravitate towards starchy carbohydrates like breads, pasta, pastries. These starchy foods tend to increase serotonin levels  in the brain which tend to calm us down, temporarily. That's why these carbohydrates are often called comfort foods. To help with stress and encourage health it would be better to mix those foods with good quality proteins. Try and eat protein with every meal and snack having between 1- 4 ounces. Rule of thumb 4 ounces is about size of half the palm of your hand. Eating protein also will actually reduce the tendency to overeat the starches and will also give you the strength

and stamina you need to manage your stress. Eating protein will help you become more bio-chemically balanced which in turn helps your body and mind function better. Protein also helps reduce the cravings for all the sweets and most foods in the snack food category. Choose high quality proteins like fish, chicken, turkey, eggs, meat, low fat cheese. Nuts, seeds and beans are not necessarily high protein foods but they do provide some of your daily allowance and are always a good alternative for vegetarians.

Also along with the protein don't forget your vegetables they contain nutrients that you body depletes quickly while under stress like Vitamin B so they need to be replenished soon so you don't feel run down and get sick. So for a well rounded include good quality protein, good fats and oils like olive oil and carbohydrates like vegetables, fruits and some grains and nuts – you will be doing yourself a big favor.

Stress Eating happens to a lot of people but you don't have to be one of them. Regardless of how many times you have used food to ease your feelings of stress in the past, you can take control starting with these easy 3 steps. It's so vital to regularly eat, high quality proteins, fats and carbohydrates this will reduce your tendency to overeat or eat the wrong unhealthy and "stress inducing foods" as we have already mentioned. Maintaining as healthy a diet as possible during stressful times is a key to good health, your weight and better state of mind. You will be more able to handle your stress and have the stamina to overcome much. Try not to judge yourself if you are not eating the best during stressful times. Be easy on yourself and proud of how well you are doing considering your circumstances. . You are not in a race but on a journey overcoming stresses, obstacles and challenges that come along your path. The journey is different for every person and you will get better at eating well and taking care of yourself - one minute, one day and year at a time. If you feel stuck in this area getting help from an expert in coaching or counseling is highly recommended.

© Monika Klein, BS, CN

You can read more about Monika Klein, BS, CN, and Coaching for Health in the Authors and Resource sections at the end of this book.

GET ORGANIZED

Clearing away unwanted stuff, including too much paperwork, can help to clear your stress.

A few timesaving and management tips to assist you in your cleaning out and organizing process:

Start right away to create a new habit of being organized – it won't happen on its own.

- ✓ Write a plan to include a list of what you will be organizing, i.e.: your desk, your cupboards, your closets, etc.
- ✓ Book specific time into your appointment calendar. Make your appointments with yourself a priority.
- ✓ To get on track, avoid promising yourself that you will do it all in one day. Most people will become overwhelmed and give up in the process. Instead spend a few minutes every day to sort, file and discard. Choose one location to clean and organize at a time, i.e.: closets, desk.

QT TO HELP YOU GET YOUR WORKSPACE

How many times have you looked for that same document or email, only to finally find it buried under several other pieces of paper, or lost in the maze of icons on your computer?

The stress of looking for it over and over can be eliminated by setting up and following a simple plan of organization.

- ✓ Keep printed documents in folders and binders for ease in finding. Create a filing system that works for you using hanging folders with plastic tabs (i.e., Pendaflex) for papers. Once you have created folders, they are available to immediately hold the paperwork you are working on as well as any related paperwork. 3 ring binders are also excellent for work in process and priority projects. In 3 ring binders you can have tabs to separate each project or idea. You can also use your 3 ring binder for only the most current and necessary information and file away all the other paperwork.

- ✓ In your computer, set up folders with the same topics and sections as your physical paper folders. Make one for each project, each client, and one for "work in progress". Set up these same folders in your email dashboard, so everything is consistent and more easily located when you need it.

- ✓ When you must print a report or notes, set your print options to print the entire file location at the bottom of the page. This saves time hunting for the file on your computer and can prevent reprinting the same information over and again.

- ✓ Stop creating more paperwork. Scan necessary paperwork into your computer files and keep it there until you need a printed copy for immediate use. Only print reports when you need them in physical form. (The exception to this is legal documents where the original is essential. In those cases set up your filing system to keep them organized.)

- ✓ When organizing and sorting through your papers and other items, ask yourself - when was the last time I used this or needed this? How important is it for me to keep? What is the worst that can happen if I get rid of it? If it is essential to keep, set up its perfect place to be and put it there now.

✓ Handle paper once – when you pick up a paper from your desk, or incoming mail – file it appropriately the first time. This way when you need it, it will be where you can find it without searching.

✓ Organize your emails. If you don't need to read it now, move it from your inbox. Having less in your inbox to weed through will make it easier to know what you need to respond to and what can wait.

   ➤ Create personal folders to organize your messages. These folders can be similar to the data folders you have crated as well as folders for your client's, friends, family, hobbies, personal, work in progress and other specifics related to your career and personal life. Keep these folders simple so you can efficiently use them and also find what you are looking for when you need it.

Use your tools and action commands to instruct your incoming mail to automatically go to the folder of your choice. This way you can read them later when you have time. This would include hobby e-zines, sales fliers, product offers and some spam. Your messages will still appear as unread, only they'll be in the folder you designated, so you can find the new ones when you click on that folder.

In outlook and other email programs, when you leave your email folders list expanded, a number in parenthesis appears next to a folder indicating how many unread emails are in the folder. You can find links to a few how-to tutorials by visiting the stress resource page at: www.stressout-book.com/stress-resources.htm

   ➤ When you respond to an email, move the original email and your sent message to the folder that you have created for those emails. If it something that required an additional response or effort, your work-in-progress folder might be appropriate

A TIP I learned from a computer geek years ago saved me when my computer crashed. Most computers have preset defaults for where your saved documents, pictures, audio and video files are saved. If your computer ever crashes (not that stress!), you will most likely need to have a technician retrieve your files. They will have to look in several places to find everywhere you saved them. And sometimes they won't be able to get to some of your most important ones. Some people save their files to their desktop and their screen is then decorated with hundreds of icons, and their desktop is disorganized after a while.

A proactive solution is to set you own file directory. Start by creating a "Data" (or name you prefer) folder on your hard drive. Under this Data folder, create folders similar to the folders you created with your paper files and email folders. Now each time you save a new file, you will be saving it to your Data section and specific folder on your hard drive. This will be a new habit to remember to save your files in their new systematic location. If you are capable of changing the default setting in your software programs, i.e.: word, excel, Photoshop, etc, you can make this even easier by letting your computer remember the new location for your files.

If your computer crashes and your have all your data files in one directory, they will be easier to locate and retrieve. And back up your information regularly onto CD's or DVD's and keep them safe.

Be sure not to move your program files or operating system files. If your computer crashes, program files and software files will usually have to be reinstalled from the original disks or downloads. Moving these command files can interfere with their function. There are several file management tutorials online to help you set up folders on your computer.

"I threw out all the papers I had been keeping from websites I'd printed to read at some other time. I made a page on my desktop of "WebPages to Visit". On the page I put the name of the website, its URL, and a quick note of what the website has that I want to read. I got rid of hundreds of papers, and it feels great." ~Brad Smorther~

"I've always used the throw-everything-in-a-box-to-be sorted-later filing system for my receipts. so when it comes time to do my taxes, I spend hours sorting and trying to remember what some of the receipts were for. Now I'm spending a certain amount of time every day sorting last years receipts so I don't get burned out. At the same time, I made myself a spreadsheet to enter my new expenses and income every day so this year I can use this spreadsheet for my taxes. I set up a special filing box with folders for each category, and before the receipt goes in the file, it's entered in the spreadsheet." ~ Marcia Bearn ~

"I cleaned my closet. Anything that I haven't worn in a year was given to charity. I cleaned my desk of saved papers and anything that isn't tax or client related, I threw away. This feels like a breath of fresh air at my desk. I can find what I need now, because it's not mixed with paperwork I no longer need." ~ Lisa Lorie ~

ℚⲦ TIPS TO ORGANIZE AROUND YOUR HOME

Studies report that when your home is disorganized or in need of cleaning it can add to your stress. Instead of being able to relax your mind is instead thinking how your home needs to be cleaned.

A once a week cleaning service can reward you with saved stress and a clean house.

These same studies report that numerous people clean their house the best only when they are expecting company, **Be your own guest**. If you are cleaning your house for company so they feel welcome, and enjoy the visit, don't you deserve the sane?! With a clean house then you can feel welcome and enjoy your time at home. It's your home, be your own guest.

A few timesaving house cleaning tips:

1. Mail. Open each item when you get it; and make a decision about it. File important letters and documents, sort bills to be pad or dispose of it. The habit of dumping all your mail in a pile to look at later, (1) your "later" will take more time, (2) you can miss important dates and deadlines, (3) if it's something you urgently need to find, it adds stress in your haste to find it.

2. Never leave a room empty handed if there is something that belongs in the room you are heading to, (i.e.: a coffee cup for the kitchen, a sweater hanging on the back of a chair that belongs in your bedroom or laundry. Take a quick glance around the room before you leave it for something that belongs in the room you are going to. And when you get into the new room resist the urge to "just set it anywhere" – put it in its place.

3. If you use a dishwasher, by pass the sink and go directly to the dishwasher. Recent health studies indicate that hand washing does not clean the dishes as completely as a dishwasher. Most dishwashers use water that is much hotter than the human hand can tolerate; plus most hand washing ends up using more water than one dishwasher load. Hand washing is an extra step and amount of time that you can save.

Additional organizing articles and tips, are included in the Stress Out Daily Tips e-zine.

PRIORITIZE YOURSELF

"There cannot be a stressful crisis next week.
My schedule is already full."
~ Henry Kissinger ~

It's so easy to get caught up in your busy lifestyle that at the end of the day you don't have time for yourself. You can get caught up in "as soon as I finish this project", or "as soon as I get the kids taken care of", or as soon as I finish _____ (fill in the blank).

During safety demonstrations on airplanes, the attendants instruct you that in the case of an emergency an oxygen mask will drop down, and if you are traveling with children or adults that need your assistance, you must put your oxygen mask on first before tending to them. If you aren't breathing, it will become more difficult if not impossible to help anyone else.

" We never know the worth of water till the well goes dry."
~ Scottish Proverb ~

Your ability to function at your best in your daily life is no different. If you are only taking care of everyone and everything else, your stress increases, your personal resources deplete and then it become more difficult to do anything. For your mental and physical health and well being, you need to make yourself a priority.

We make appointments with people and events we feel are important, i.e. doctors, dentists, clients, hairdresser, our spouses and kid's events. We even make sure to take time to set the television DVR. Taking care of everyone else first and giving more importance to other people and ignoring yourself damages your feelings of self worth and self esteem.

- ❖ Acknowledge that YOU are important and start making appointments with yourself.
- ❖ Make appointments with yourself in your calendar.
- ❖ If you use a written calendar, write your appointment with yourself in ink, don't pencil it in,
- ❖ If you use an online calendar , such as Google, or a calendar such as Outlook or Outlook Express, set timers to remind you of your appointments with yourself.
- ❖ And when your appointment time arrives – keep it.

If you have difficulty setting appointments with yourself, start small with 5 minutes and build up time to 15, 30 or 60 minutes.

- ❖ Set an appointment with yourself to read something inspirational or humorous
- ❖ Set an appointment with yourself to meditate
- ❖ Set an appointment with yourself to write thank you notes
- ❖ Set an appointment with yourself to exercise
- ❖ Set an appointment with yourself to call a friend
- ❖ Set an appointment with yourself for pampering

❖ Set an appointment with yourself to watch or listen to something funny – and laugh.

❖ Set an appointment with yourself to take a walk in nature

❖ Set an appointment for something that you have been putting off that you really want to do.

The Stress Out Daily Tips free e-zine will offer additional time management tips so you can set more appointment times with yourself.

DELEGATE

"The best executive is the one who has sense enough
to pick good people to do what he wants done,
and self-restraint enough
to keep from meddling with them while they do it."
~ Theodore Roosevelt ~

Everybody has days when there simply seems there's too much work to get done. Trying to get everything done by yourself can really bring on stress. Some people effectively deal with the pressure by learning how to delegate certain jobs to others. When you unburden yourself and not worry about every detail of how the work gets done, if you can put full faith and trust in someone else to assist you it can be an effective escape valve.

Some people can't let go. If you have the type of personality that demands to know how things are going every minute, chances are you're only increasing the pressure and stress on yourself with this constantly worrying.

To lessen stress you must either learn to trust others to get the job done, or prioritize jobs to get rid of "what must be done" first or not at all.

8 Really, Really Good Reasons to Hire a Virtual Assistant

Really, Really Good Reason #1: I'd rather be dancing....NOT trying to figure out the nuances of audio acrobat.

Really, Really Good Reason #2: YOU need to be wearing a $150 to $250 per hour "Fashion Statement" hat --- NOT a $25 to $55 per hour hat.

Really, Really Good Reason #3: Why should you spend 7 to 15 hours (or more!) researching target markets, figuring out a software package, setting up a teleconference call and bridge line, or updating your website with "links" and html codes? Your Virtual Assistant can accomplish the same amount of work in 3 to 4 hours @ $25 per hour? YOU need to be either on the phone coaching or networking in the flesh --- as your VA is unable to do either one. For $100, your VA is able to put you in "front" of 15 prospects who can then "click, click, click" away on your "Contact Me" page!

Really, Really Good Reason #4: We did NOT start our own businesses so we could continue trading our "time" for "money". We started our own businesses so we could be paid for the value we bring to the client, the experience we bring to the client, and the results we bring to the client. When we do this, the client will never equate us to an 'hourly' rate. How much is the "light at the end of the tunnel" worth? That is something YOU decide; not the client and not the clock!

Really, Really Good Reason #5: You want to have the time to "re-purpose" every really good idea you come up with. If you write a brilliant article, your VA can help you turn it into a CD or a workbook or a seminar. Let the VA help you make sales while you sleep. That's "leveraging" at the utmost level of pleasure!

Really, Really Good Reason #6: You should be doing what you LOVE to do and flowing in your gifts as much as possible. So, if you LOVE to coach --- coach! If you LOVE to write --- you can write and coach! If you LOVE to speak --- you can speak and coach! If you LOVE to update websites --- be a web designer! (I hope you get the point!) I have had great success in delegating ad campaigns to my VA. So, if you either can't write or dislike writing --- a VA can create the content for you and post it, too. If it's a "struggle", "not your gig", or worth $25 to $55 per hour --- OUTSOURCE IT!

Really, Really Good Reason #7: Lots and lots of money can be made from affiliate programs and joint ventures. It takes lots and lots of hours to determine which ones are worth partnering with. YOU do NOT have the time for this. YOU make the most money when you are actually coaching or speaking. But, you can make a sweet passive income as an affiliate partner with a well-established coach with a BIG LIST! So, again, allow your VA to research the myriad of affiliate programs and let him or her report back to you the ones worth considering. Remember, it could take you months to dig up this buried treasure. A good VA will probably already know who the big players are and how to hook you up! Then, the VA can register you with that Big Fish, throw the affiliate link onto your website and watch your bank account grow!

Really, Really Good Reason #8: It's totally un-cool to be a control freak. Build a team so you can control only your time and enjoy both the ride and the destination.

© Debra Costanzo.

You can learn more about Debra Costanzo and 3 in 1 Fitness in the Author section in the back of this book.

JOB STRESS

Job stress occurs when you work too much; work in conflict with your values and talents or work under difficult circumstances. It is not news to anyone that stress can make you physically sick.

Not only can work stress make you sick, but also once you get sick, your lower energy levels affect the quality and quantity of your work. Eventually, impaired performance can ruin your career.

Whether you work for yourself, own a business or are an employee, stress on the job is a growing problem. With increasing financial constraints, employers are asking more of each worker with fewer resources. You are not only concerned about your stress, but also the stress of the people around you. Other's stress can affect your work and health as well.

In this chapter, we will explore the underlying cause for stress, how take charge of your stress and some of the arenas of work life that can be stressful and strategies to reduce stress in each of them. At the end, there are also suggested resources to support you in handling work stress.

KEY CAUSE OF STRESS

Take a moment to write down a few of the things that stress you at work. Look at the items on your list. What do the items all have in common? Do you have control over any of them?

Situations that cause you stress are situations you feel you cannot control – too much to do with too little time or resources, other people not pulling their load, negative or demanding supervisors or coworkers, or fear of job loss for example.

The key to reducing your stress is focusing your time and energy on the things within your control, namely your own thoughts, feelings and choices within the situation.

THE KEY PRINCIPLE FOR STRESS REDUCTION

- You have NO control of anything outside yourself.
- You have TOTAL control of everything inside yourself.

This does not seem earth-shattering until you look at daily reactions to what stresses you.

You reduce your stress when you put your time and energy into the one area where it will pay off, where you have total control and power to direct your life – in YOU, what you think, feel and choose (your actions). This brings you the confidence and freedom of Self-Mastery.

Keeping this principle in mind will serve you well as you learn to reduce your stress in any area of your life, including your work life.

ARENAS OF STRESS AT WORK

The following are some typical arenas of work stress in which you can reclaim more control.

PURPOSE

"Follow your bliss."
~ Joseph Campbell ~

Are you stressed by feeling stuck in a job situation that does not allow expression of your true talents and abilities? Are you working in an area you hate because you have been there so long it is hard to leave or you need the money? This is a huge cause for work related stress.

Purpose is a force that energizes. It inspires you to get up in the morning. What excites your passion for work? Your deepest values and purpose are not in your head but in your heart. To what does your heart respond? What touches you? What energizes you or inspires you?

When you follow your true path or calling, you are invigorated, rather than stressed.

I'm reminded of a story about a man who purchased a quarry. He didn't know anything about the quarry business. So, on the first day the new owner decided to learn about the work done there. He asked an industrious worker what he was doing. The worker replied, "I am making bricks. They must be exactly the right size, so I use a special mold to shape them with precision." The owner then asked a second worker who was also busy making bricks, "What is it that you do here?" The worker said, "I make a living. By working here I put food on the table and support my growing family." When the owner proceeded to ask the third worker the same question, the worker smiled broadly, "I am building a cathedral!" he said with enthusiasm.

The sense of doing something valuable and purposeful can change your outlook.

Action Steps:

✓ Define your job by its larger benefit to the world. Take the person who recently put in a phone jack for my computer for instance. This was a routine task for him, but that work connects me to the entire world through the Internet capability it provides. This man's job is not just the installation of phone connections; he actually facilitates worldwide communication.

After a recent presentation on this subject, a woman remarked to me, "I really expedite interoffice communication which enhances the relationships in the entire organization." This woman previously saw herself as "just a secretary". Once she expanded her view of the outcome of her work, she could see how what she did routinely made a significant difference in the overall quality of work life for everyone. Now, she feels excited about her contribution! Knowing that you make an important difference helps you to feel valuable inside, even when you rarely hear the words "Thank You" from your boss, co-workers, or customers.

Look at the outcome of your work. How would the workplace change if you were not there? Focus not only on the tasks, but also on what you personally contribute because of your unique abilities and personality.

Inspire yourself with a broader vision of your contribution to the world. Find the cathedral hidden in your job.

✓ Get career counseling or coaching to identify your strengths and talents, and then set a plan in motion to attract a position either within your current organization or in another. Once you are clear on your ideal position, communicate your interests. Frequently, you will begin to see or hear about situations that could be a good fit for you.
✓ Check with your organization's Human **Resources** department to determine if there are opportunities for education, training or career development available for which you may qualify.

BURNOUT

After forty years specializing in stress and burnout, one thing is clear to me. Burnout is the result of people working in conflict with their deepest values over time. While physical stress is tiring, the spiritual stress of being out of harmony with your truth, your values, is devastating.

What is the most important value you hold about your work? Is it connecting with and helping other people? Is it doing a quality job? Do you hold strong values for honesty, integrity, personal growth...? Think about the day when you came home exhausted and yet felt good inside about something you did or experienced. What is it that stands out in your mind at those moments that make them special to you?

In workshops, I ask nurses to draw a picture of what nursing is about for them. Rarely do those pictures contain pills, IVs, charts or even hospital beds. Nearly all the pictures contain hearts, hands clasped with one another, smiling faces, symbols of connection between human beings. This is what nurses value most. When they have to focus most of their time on record keeping and paperwork, they are out of alignment with their deepest values. Over time, burnout is inevitable.

Action Steps

✓ Take time to identify your deep values and think about how you can align with living your values more at work. Is there a way to alter or change your work situation to be more aligned with your values? This is an area where talking the situation over with a trusted advisor might be helpful.

✓ Are you selling something you don't believe in, being asked to lie to clients or customers or have other demands like this that conflict with your values? You may need to be assertive with your employer and let them know this is not an acceptable requirement.

✓ If you cannot change the situation internally to the organization, you may want to begin searching for another work situation. The stress of working outside your values can be particularly devastating to your mental and physical health over time.

TIME PRESSURE

Choosing consciously what you do in this moment is the most powerful and least stressful thing you can do. There is a finite amount of time in a day. You control what you choose to do with it.

Prioritizing what is most important is essential. Then, it is easier to see what must either be delegated or dropped from the "to do" list. Life becomes simpler, less stressful and more productive when you are realistic about what you can do and take responsibility for acting on that priority in the present moment.

Action Steps

✓ Ask yourself frequently, "What is the best use of my time right now?"

✓ Take time to evaluate antiquated systems and streamline processes. The resources needed to maintain old cumbersome systems are simply not available today. For example, create a team made up of members of different departments within the organization who depend upon the same information to discuss ways to streamline the paperwork or share the information electronically more efficiently. Ask questions like, "If we were designing this process from scratch, what would it look like? What elements are essential and which ones are vestiges that consume precious time and resources without a substantial return.

✓ Make choices based upon immediate priorities. List your priorities at the beginning of the day and label them "A" for top priority, "B" for important and not urgent and "C" for routine tasks. Focus on your "A" priorities first and see where you can delegate the B & C tasks.

✓ Only handle each piece of mail or paper once. Decide as soon as you pick it up whether to act on it, delegate it, file it or discard it. The less you go back to each piece of paper the less time you will waste.

✓ Batch tasks. When you do the same task repeatedly, you increase your speed and efficiency. For example, attend to e-mail at specific times of the day and do not attend to it in between, batch your return phone calls to do right before lunch or end of the day when possible because people will tend to stick to the subject and get off the phone at those times.

JOB SECURITY

What will happen to my company? Will it be in business? Will I have a job? Questions like these are rampant in today's workplace. As bad news and fear spreads it can become a self-fulfilling prophesy. While the future is not in your control, you can use these tips to take charge of job security concerns.

Action Steps

✓ Be proactive. Continuously update your resume or job portfolio.

✓ Be aware of expanding and new markets for your talents and skills. You do not need to leave your job or take any particular action. Just focusing your time and energy on productive preparation rather than wasteful worrying will reduce your stress.

✓ You can also find ways to increase your value to the bottom line of your current job. Where can you help shave costs and increase profits in your work area? What value added services or products can you create? Putting your energy into proactively adding value to yourself or your job helps you stand out from the crowd as an asset to your organization and in your portfolio. Over time, your organization may even reward your actions and ideas with additional monetary or positional compensation.

OTHER PEOPLE

The most difficult stressor for most of us is other people.

We often blame other people for our feelings, thoughts and the choices we feel forced to make. The truth is other people are not responsible for any of these things. When you give others control over your feelings, thoughts and choices, you feel powerlessly stressed.

The natural response to loss of control or the fear of loss is fight, flight or freeze. It's no surprise that as more people feel out of control in their lives, incidents of rage (fight), depression (flight) and chronic illness (freeze) are increasing.

Each human being is unique. This fact is borne out in our DNA, voice patterns and fingerprints. We express that uniqueness in how we interpret our experience of the world from birth to death.

When you understand that just like you, others have the equal right to think, feel and act according to their own judgment and that they have unique perspectives, you realize that trying to control another person is futile.

In de-stressing a relationship, you are concerned about not only your stress but also the stress of the other person. You want to reduce the fear of loss of control on both sides of the relationship.

Standing in your power to control your side of the relationship is your right and responsibility. At the same time, creating an environment where others know you are respecting their equal rights and responsibility for their unique side of the communication has the potential to reduce their stress as well.

Agreement is not the basis for stress-free relationships. The basis for healthy relationships is respect, freedom and value of each unique person for the other's equal freedom and right to think, feel, make personal choices and take responsibility for them.

When others are hostile, angry, complaining or negative, you can take control by setting some boundaries for yourself in the relationship. Leave the space when possible, or be assertive about what you will and will not discuss. Especially put limits on gossiping about others.

When someone is shouting at you or venting their negative feelings and you cannot create distance here is a visualization you can use to protect yourself and your feelings.

ℚ꓄ TRASH BAG TECHNIQUE:

Imagine you have a huge plastic trash bag in front of you. Imagine the person's negative or hostile words dropping right into the bag. Do not take their words into yourself. Once the venting is over, imagine the garbage truck pulling up, put the bag into the truck and watch it leave.

When you have emotional stress from the behaviors, attitudes or beliefs of other people, one of the most effective techniques to use is the Emotional Freedom Technique (EFT). This simple acupressure technique works instantly to reduce your reaction. When your reaction is under control, you can think more clearly and take appropriate action. You can find more information on this in the resources section of this book.

Ask for feedback and clarification. Realize that people tend to fill in the blanks from their own perspective and don't realize that they are not communicating clearly, until a breakdown in communication has occurred. You can minimize the stress of miscommunications by seeking and offering feedback. For example, ask people when you delegate a task, how they understood instructions. This will give you a chance to clarify any misconceptions quickly.

ENVIRONMENT

We live and work in sealed environments, breathing recirculated air for long periods. Much of our air and water contains chemicals and we are supposed to stay out of the sun or add chemical barriers to our skin to protect us from the vital rays we need.

Working long hours in sedentary jobs, watching television and over stimulating our system with caffeine, sugar and other chemicals can create sleep deprivation and fatigue.

All these conditions stress the body and mind.

Living in the world requires attention and conscious choice to give your body what it needs to stay well. Your body is amazing! It has its own self-repair mechanisms and does not require perfect resources to be well. Movement in the right direction will do wonders.

Action Steps

✓ When you breathe, you inspire. When you do not breathe, you expire. Taking a deep breath periodically during the day can measurably reduce your stress. So can eating regular meals and drinking purified water. These are some of the simple steps to reclaiming control of your physical stress.

✓ Stress is an energy vibration. You can reduce your stress by using other vibrations that are either soothing or enjoyable to you. Color, sound, odors, images all have vibrations. Which vibrations resonate with you in a way that soothes, energizes or affects your mood?

✓ When you can, paint the walls of your office with color that supports your energy; add images, sounds, textures and fragrances you love. Then observe how you feel in the space you have created.

✓ If you cannot go out, at least look out a window periodically. If there isn't a window available, put a part of nature in your space, like flowers, water, seashells, rocks or even a photo of nature. When you are out of touch with the natural world, it is easy to lose perspective.

✓ Reconnecting with nature is a way to helps you feel more alive and centered. This not only reduces stress but increases energy and vitality.

✓ What kinds of sounds do you listen to all day long? Are you exposed to noise pollution? Do you hear the sounds of motors whirring, phones ringing, people arguing or other sounds that irritate your senses?

✓ When you are around the same sounds all the time, you tend to tune them out of awareness. Even though these sounds are outside of your awareness, their vibrations still affect you. Consider adding a fountain, soft music or other enjoyable background sounds to your workspace.

Additional Resources

Your workplace Employee Assistance Program (EAP) or Employee Health Program are excellent resources to help you reduce work stress. If you do not have access to these programs, consider investing in counseling or coaching to regain control over your stress.

You may also want to consider:
** Career coaching for taking control of your portfolio and exploring career options
** Assertiveness classes for learning how to communicate with clarity and decisiveness
** Emotional Freedom Technique classes or coaching

© Aila Accad, RN, MSN.

You can learn more about Aila Accad, RN, MSN in the Author and Resource sections at the end of this book.

WRITE YOUR OWN PERSONAL SELF HELP BOOK

Self help books have been around for dozens of years. As early as 360AD Epictetus wrote extensively about self discipline as a means to control the outcomes in your life. In 1892, Thomas J. Hudson, PhD talked about harnessing the power we have within us, and 1905 Wallace D. Wattles, who is more recently known as the inspiration for the movie The Secret, wrote about how we can help ourselves have a richer, life. In the early 1900's Annie Besant wrote about expanding your happiness though self knowledge. Charles F. Haanel, RHJ, Emmet Fox, and Earl Nightingale wrote books of detailed information that encouraged readers to expand their possibilities, set higher goals and build upon their self confidence.

My first introduction to self help was through the book Think and Grow Rich by Napoleon Hill, which is still used by countless people to help them to make changes in their personal and professional lives. I have seen the message in Hill's book repeated in several other authors' books over the years.

Each year more books and videos hit the shelves. Each one of them is saying the same thing, perhaps with a few different words, maybe with a different tool and with a different delivery – however, the message of helping yourself is the same. Most adults today have read quite a collection of self help books. Their books now contain dog eared pages and highlighted sentences of specific words which spoke to them at a deep, soul level. These are special books, and they never are lent out to anyone.

If you have a library of only a few books, you were drawn to your books, and the sections you highlighted initially because some part of you knew that these were answers you were seeking. Whether you followed the advice or simply highlighted throughout the book and sent it aside, these phrases meant something to you at that time, and they can again.

Use your own inspiration to guide you to your stress solutions. Select one book at a time. Find only the highlighted portions and then transfer these phrases, words and sentences into your journal or a word document on your computer. Include your handwritten notes from the margins and the quotes that inspired you.

Next include all the notes from any workshop or class you have taken.

What you are creating is your own personal self help book. These are the answers that you keep seeking. Amongst the words and pages in all these books, these answers may appear lost; however, when you bring them together into one book, you will be able to see your inspiration and answers more clearly.

You may discover new ideas, be reminded of tools you already possess and even if these books have been collecting dust on your shelves for a long time, they might now hold the action steps you are ready for today.

QT **Remember the Highlights**

Prior to starting your own personal self help book, you can gain benefit with each single book. Select one of your favorite books from the shelf and read only the highlighted and underlined sections. Continue skimming the book only reading your specially selected portions. As you read and remember why these words spoke to you in the first place your energy will also remember how you felt when you were first inspired by this book and its message. The more inspired you become, the less you will be stressed. Science has proven that you can only one thing at a time can hold a space. You can only hold one emotion or one thought at a time. Be inspired again.

RECOGNIZE YOUR STRENGTH

"What doesn't kill you makes you stronger."
~ Friedrich Nietzsche ~

This is one of my least favorite quotes. Nietzsche is credited for writing this quote in the 19th century. As an existentialist philosopher much of his work was focused on interpreting tragedy as an affirmation of life. This quote was one of his explanations of his ability to overcome his ill-health and often intense physical pain. Nietzsche conducted a substantial amount of research on attitudes, personal convictions and motivations. Much of his work is said to have been an inspiration to Sigmund Freud's development of psychoanalysis and is still being referred to today. I read that he also proclaimed that "God is Dead". Interestingly, it is reported that he suffered from mental illness most of his adult life; reportedly suffering a mental breakdown from which he never recovered and was declared insane just prior to his death. So the question is, did his difficulties make him stronger or was it the weight of these difficulties that contributed to his mental deterioration?

My research and the answers I received from the many people who responded to my polls simply add to my bewilderment at the popularity of this quote. It has been said so often that it has become iconic. Based on the many poll responses, this phrase is an empty and flippant platitude when you're feeling stressed about something in your life.

You already possess the strength within you however; it has been clouded over with all the past statements of fear and stress. It's still there, it simply needs to be re-exposed and re-claimed by you. Just like throwing mud all over yourself doesn't eliminate you underneath, you just can't be seen under all mud. You simply need to remove the mud to find yourself again.

If you are like most people, you have certain statements that consistently run through your mind and pepper your conversations. The repetition of these statements give them power and you eventually live your life by them, whether they are true or not.

When these statements tell you that you are powerless or inadequate, or that you lack the resources to handle whatever is happening in your life, you then feel powerless and inadequate. When these statements are a repeat of a stressful event or fear, they sap your energy and make it difficult for you to find your strength to deal with whatever is actually happening in the present moment.

Many therapists, coaches and workshop leaders emphasize the importance of getting these negative, energy draining statements out of your mind, your thoughts and your conversations. One way is to write them out on paper. Actually seeing the words in print helps you to observe, in your reactions, how untrue and damaging they are. Following your writing out the negative and untrue statements with a reaffirming one will give you something new and powerful to support you. When you let go of an old statement, a void is created, so something new must replace it. The affirmations you wrote from the exercise in a previous chapter can be beneficial in this exercise as well.

For this exercise you need several pieces of blank paper, a pencil and a black felt tip pen. The actual hand to paper touch and movement, and seeing your hand doing this, is a significant part of letting go and reaffirming your strength.

Take your first sheet of paper and using a **dull PENCIL**, begin writing down all of those stressful statements that you have listened to so many times in the past; those messages you have heard echo in your mind for so long that you mistakenly believe they are the truth. All those statements that you have been telling yourself that you cannot find a solution, you don't have the strength or resources, you aren't smart enough, know enough, or anything similar that makes you feel like stress is controlling your life. Include the statements of why is this happening, or it's someone else's fault or any other statement that makes you feel like giving up.

Keep writing as fast as you can.

When the paper appears full, turn it **upside down, same side up** and keep writing. Now you are writing over your previously written sentences.

Keep writing every reason why you can't have, can't be, all the should's and should not's. Let your handwriting be sloppy, let your grammar be whatever it is and keep writing. No one other than you is going to see this. Keep writing, even if its "this is stupid", or "I don't believe this will work for me" (Two statements shared by people I spoke with regarding the first time they did this exercise. Their opinion has changed).

When the paper appears full again, turn the page **sideways** and keep writing. **Same side of the paper**. Keep writing until these thoughts run out. If you run out of room, turn the paper sideways again and keep writing. You are only using one side of this paper even when all you can see is more pencil that clean paper.

If you have never used this technique in the past, it may seem like a long process when it is actually only a few minutes. Keep your commitment keep writing and emptying these words onto the paper. It is important to empty your mind so you can start clean.

When your mind is done chattering, put down the pencil and pick up a dark, thick **BLACK FELT TIP PEN**.

Start at the top of you paper which is covered in pencil writings, and using your **black felt tip pen**, start writing your affirmations and strong statements about yourself one line at a time. Write clearly and completely over the pencil writings. Write larger and bolder with your black felt tip pen, so you can clearly see your statements.

These statements are opposite of what you wrote in pencil. These include any affirmations you wrote in the affirmations chapter. Include statements of how capable you are, how smart you are, how resilient you are, how trustworthy you are. Remember times when you **did** find a solution to a problem, overcame something you originally thought you wouldn't, bounced back from a stressful event or circumstance. Write the opposite of the negative and energy draining statements you wrote in pencil.

Breathe fully, using the support of your diaphragm and feel your inner strength.

When you use your black felt tip pen to write over the top of your previous pencil statement, the pencil writings will fade in the background, and the black pen statements will become predominant on the page. This way, all you can see when you are done, is your strength, your capabilities, everything positive about you – **BOLDLY!**

Continue writing your BOLD declarations until the page is full, then **take out another piece of clean paper and keep writing**. Or start writing these Bold statements into a personal journal. Fill both sides of the sheets of clean paper. Use as many pieces of paper as necessary. Keep writing until all you can think about is what you are writing in **Bold Black ink.**

When you are finished, you will have pages of strong bold declarations. You can keep the loose pages of bold statements in a binder, or re-read your journal of bold statements to remind you. Your pencil page with bold overwriting is a visual that your bold statements are more powerful.

After doing this writing and release, it is important to get up and move your body. Put on music you enjoy and move to it, or take a short walk, or shake out your arms and legs. Find the physical release that works for you.

This is one powerful method of re-phrasing and re-training your conscious and subconscious mind. This is redirecting your focus onto your strengths and capabilities.

You can always just write out a page of bold declarations; however that activity can be compared to putting clean water into glass already filled with dirty water. If you keep the clean water running long enough, eventually the dirty water will become more and clearer. On the other hand, emptying the dirty water out of the glass first before putting in clean water will make it easier and faster to have a glass full of clean water. If you leave the water in the glass alone to sit undisturbed and with no clean water coming in, it will become stagnant again from the residual "dirt" in the original dirty glass or it can pick up dirt from outside influences. You must keep the clean flow of water going in to continually clean out the dirt. The same is true for your mind. You must use this technique EVERY TIME you begin to hear your statements being more stressful than empowering and you start to feel your strength again becoming muddied over.

Each time you do this exercise you are reinforcing your capabilities, your personal power and strength. You are opening your mind to possibilities, creative thinking and solutions to the stressful events and circumstances in your life.

"Whatever a person's mind dwells on intensely
and with firm resolve,
that is exactly what they become."
~ Shankaracharya ~

LANDING SUNNY SIDE UP

"Adopting the right attitude
can convert a negative stress into a positive one."
~ Hans Selye ~

Anyone who has lived knows that we will encounter adversity during our lives. I am no different.

I have discovered five ways that help me to land sunny side up.

1. Reframe things – Choosing to look at any situation in a positive light can be very challenging, but it is a power we all posses. Feeling empowered is so important to our healing and recovery process. Sometimes you just need to dig down and find the sunny spot.

2. Create happy space – Feeding our senses can help us get happy when sheer force of will isn't enough. I'm all for the little black dress, but color has a large impact on our moods. Start by putting on something brightly colored and listen to music that lifts your spirits. You can feel devastated and still dance.

3. Allow grief some time – Acknowledging our feelings allows them to pass through more quickly. Even if you are

doing steps one and two, it's okay to admit to feeling unhappiness too. This too shall pass.

4. Gratitude list – I find that making a daily list of 5 things I am grateful for helps to lighten my world and nothing succeeds like success. This is a very simple, but extremely powerful tool to help you through anything life dishes out.

5. Help others – Service to others helps us feel useful, happy. Being able to do something, anything when we feel most helpless is a tonic to us and a great help to others in need.

None of us are strangers to life's difficulties, and stressors, but with some simple awareness and realization of our interconnectedness we can all help each other get through with smiles on our faces.

© Gina Cotroneo.

You can learn more about Gina Cotroneo and her Soul's Calling products in the Author and Resource sections at the end of this book.

ROAD RAGE

Anyone who's ever been stuck in a major traffic jam probably has seen the darker side of many people's personalities including their own. It seems today that everyone is always in a hurry to either get, or go somewhere, and with so many people it doesn't seem possible to escape the traffic problems that are bound to crop up from time to time.

You may have started out at the right time, with best intentions of arriving easily at your destination; or you left late and are attempting to catch up time by speeding and hurrying down the road. With so many people more people driving, the roads are getting more and more crowded.

People cutting you off, some with hand signals; traffic accidents blocking the road and causing detours; lookie-loos slowing down to get a better eye full of the accident; slow drivers; tailgaters. None of which is ever you of course, and you never deserve those traffic tickets either. So even though it may appear as if everyone else decided to get on the road the same time as you, just to get in your way and irritate you, the reality is that you are possibly someone else's irritation too.

You can make lots of plans, and use relaxation tools in advance of getting into your car, but – now you're in it - now what?!

Banging on the steering wheel, laying on the horn, giving someone the "finger" or shooting a string of obscenities is only reacting to something that has already happened. You can't make the guy in front of you go any faster, or prevent someone from cutting you off. Accidents, road repairs, and just plain heavy traffic happens. You may not realize it, but how you act on your way to work or on your way home will have either a positive or negative impact on the time that follows and your stress level.

For your emotional health and physical safety you must learn positive ways to deal with traffic or cease driving. Although you cannot control traffic, you can control your behaviors and choices.

In most cities you have choices. Consider changing your route from time to time. Although in some areas, it may seem like every route is clogged with heavy traffic, sometimes the scenery can make a difference.

Consider taking the Metro, train, bus or carpool. Let someone else do the driving for you. This may not be glamorous, especially in cities where a person considers their car as an extension of their personality, however, you will look better in that convertible when you are healthy. Traveling by these alternate methods gives you time to relax, read a book and meet new friends. It is also much safer to do certain personal activities while riding in one of these vehicles than in your car anyway.

Don't drink and drive. This is not only about alcohol; it is about hot coffee too. If you are afraid of spilling your hot coffee in your lap while you drive, your attention is not fully on the road and you become a hazard to yourself and other drivers.

Wear your seatbelt – correctly. Not only is this the law, it has a psychological effect on your driving. If you get on the road with the attitude "I hate seatbelts, I hate this law", you are taking your anger on the road. If you "forget" to put on you seatbelt, you are most likely not paying attention to other important parts of your driving either. There are arguments both for and against wearing seatbelts, however, the fact remains – it is a law is most states and the fines can be costly. Not to mention the time you lose by being stopped or not wearing one.

There are other things that you can control while you are driving to keep stress out of the driver's seat:

🚗 Breathe. How are you breathing when you drive? Do you chest breathe or breathe fully with the support of your diaphragm? If you have developed into a chest breather when you drive, start now to retrain yourself to fully breathe. Practice a few deep abdominal breaths before starting your car and getting on the road. Check your breathing while you drive.

🚗 Seat Placement. If you too close or too far away from the steering wheel and the pedals you are adding stress to yourself as you drive. Although to some, this comment may seem obvious, you can see drivers on the road poised within inches of their steering wheel or those steering with their arms fully and uncomfortably extended towards the steering wheel.

🚗 Posture. Where are your shoulders? Do your ears appear to be closer to your shoulders than usual? Some people hold so tightly on the steering wheel without even noticing that they are tightening their shoulders and compressing their chest. Take in a full breathe and straighten your posture. Shrug your shoulders and relax them. Even if you are holding your hands on the 10 and 2 marks on your steering wheel, you can still keep your shoulders and arms relaxed. Check your seat for lumbar support. During prolonged driving your lumbar can lose its curve, and lack of lumbar support can lead to back problems. If your car isn't equipped with a lumbar support that fits your back, there are several after market products available.

🚗 Stop Talking. Millions of people have a belief that they cannot drive without talking on a cell phone, and the also believe that they are able to talk endlessly without any distraction to their ability to drive. Yet there are numerous poll results that show how much distraction cell phones cause, which has led many states to pass laws against talking on a cell phone without a headset. Even with a headset, talking on a cell phone is distracting and can be stressful. You arrive at your destination more tense, which means you must have been driving more tense when talking on the phone. Avid cell phone users will argue this information, however, test it out for yourself. Drive for a few days without talking on your cell phone and observe how differently you feel during your drive and when you get to your destination.

Listen to yourself. What are you saying aloud and to yourself? Are you cursing the other drivers, angry at yourself for being late, ruminating about something that happened before you got in the car? Are your words making you angry, happy, fearful, relaxed or stressed? Change your thoughts and your words and you can change how you are feeling. Sing a song instead.

Check your outside influences. What are you listening to? It has been proven that the music we listen to influences our emotions and physical responses in both in good and bad ways. If you are feeling angry or stressed as you drive, the music you listen to can increase those feelings or help you to relax. Certain music was written specifically to excite you and other music was recorded for easier listening. You don't need to listen to "elevator" tunes when you drive, however, observe how the music you listen to affects how you are feelings. When you consciously observe your reactions, you may need to change your tunes for a few minutes or for the full drive. Talk shows and news only stations can be distracting. If you find yourself in congested traffic, these shows may not be the best option at that time when your full attention is needed on the road.

ℚᴛ **JUST SCREAM**

One particular day when I was feeling very overtired and stressed out from too many things going on in my life all at the same time, I was also feeling some physical pain. A friend had suggested that I see a chiropractor to release the pressure in my body and have a body re-alignment. She went on to suggest that if I were to have this done on a regular basis, I would probably be able to handle things with a different approach.

Never having been to a chiropractor before, I was not sure what to expect. I am not a doctor person by nature and going to see a chiropractor seemed like a waste of my time. I do not like being poked and prodded. But, I went anyway, just to find out what a doctor who did not know anything about me could do, or suggest, to take away my pain. I was going to be open minded and accept whatever he suggested as a sincere attempt at whatever it was that needed to be done to relieve the pain once and for all.

As with any new patient, there were a number of forms that needed to be filled out which, I thought were unnecessary. I kept thinking to myself, "How is all this information going to take away my stress and my pain?" Finally, the nurse called my name and showed me a room. After waiting what seemed to be forever, the doctor entered the room and introduced himself. The doctor turned out to be rather nice and after a brief discussion as to why I was there, he said "OK, now let's just check out your back." He indicated that my back was out of alignment, my shoulders and neck muscles were tight, and that an adjustment was in order. For a split second I thought, "This is good, we are both on the same page" He suggested that I lie face down on the table and explained what was about to happen. Pressure, which was put on my spine through a few hand adjustments, was supposed to put my back bones back into place, and realign my spine back to its normal position. He also did a quick twist to my neck. I thought for sure at that point my head was going to leave my body. He said, "Just relax now, as I get your neck back into its proper position. The noise I perceived as bones cracking in my neck, (which really didn't happen) was a new experience for me.

After my major overhaul, he said something which never occurred to me before. He said, "Beverly, sales is a stressful job as you know, so I want you to try something which I think will help you get rid of some of that stress. At least once everyday, I want you to scream. "You can scream into a pillow, in your car, or at home if it is easier for you. This exercise has to last 5 minutes long and must be done very slowly. So you will have to repeat it a few times in a row. You start by pretending that you are an opera singer. You are going to scream at the top of your lungs.

You start this by taking a few deep breaths in and slowly exhale. Then take in a real deep breath and chose one word to scream as you are exhaling very slowly. Try to make this last at least 20 seconds and then see if you can work it up slowly to one minute.

Hum.... I thought. And this is going to help me how? He went on to say, "this can take away most of that built up stress which stays bottled up inside you after a long day. If you end up in traffic, turn on your radio to an opera or classical music station and just sing LOUDLY along with person on the radio." "Make sure it is not rock n' roll, hard rock or heavy metal. Just breathe in, and as you exhale, screaming one word, slowly and repeat this exercise over again until you feel your stress level feels lowered. Then come back in a week and let me know how it went. I thanked the doctor for his advice and went on my way.

On the way home I ended up stuck in traffic. I was on the 405, one of the busiest freeways in LA. I started to feel stressed again because I had to be at an appointment and did not want to be late. Here is a chance to put that opera screaming into good use I thought. "OK," I instructed myself, "breathe in slowly and exhale slowly."

Now the next step. Breathe in slowly, and this time exhale slowly and scream out one word making it last 20 seconds. I clocked the first attempt on my watch with its second hand. "This is harder than it sounds I thought."

Then looking in the mirror, as the traffic came to a complete stop, I noticed my face was turning red. Hum...I wondered, was this a good thing? or was I ready to pass out? I waited a few more seconds until I felt a little more confident, and tried the procedure again. This time it was not as hard to do, however, the 20 seconds still felt like they were never going to end and could not come soon enough.

After a few more tries, I felt I was in more control over my experience. The trick, I learned was that I had to stop and regroup letting my body relax in between each long drawn out exhaled scream or shall I say fine tuning of my vocal cords.

This exercise did work for me and could work for someone else too. I felt it was a very good prescription on the doctor's part as I was prepared to come home with a written prescription or told to take some aspirin instead. But, now I was given a tool which put me in control over this cure. I still use this exercise today and have shared the information with a number of friends. Who ever thought that listening to opera would be a cure for my stress?

I must say that this was a very good exercise for me to fulfill.

I learned that I can sing even if it is off key.

I do not always need a prescription from the Pharmacy to relieve my pain.

And going to the chiropractor was not such a bad experience after all.

There are many physical ailments and symptoms that most Chiropractors treat. If you are considering visiting a chiropractor, ask your friends or your medical doctor for a referral and do your research for information to understand the treatments.

© Beverly Edelstein

You can learn more about Beverly Edelstein in the Author Section in the back of this book,

Zzzzzzzz

Get enough sleep

It is no secret that the everyday stress of life, work, family and other commitments can wear someone out. But what do you do when all you want to do is get some rest, but you can't fall asleep or stay asleep? According to a National Sleep survey, almost half (48 percent) of Americans report lying awake at night due to stress.

I had trouble sleeping, not from my thoughts but from the constant ringing in my ears. My doctor diagnosed it as tinnitus and offered me medication to lessen it. The medication not only didn't work, I felt nauseous when I took it. I felt I was doomed to hear this disturbing noise every night. I tried white noise machines and soft music, but they couldn't drown out the ringing in my ears. Some nights were worse than others. One night when I couldn't sleep, I landed upon a medical show on TV and they were discussing tinnitus and some of the potential causes and habits that made it worse. Although the cause of mine has never been diagnosed, I took notes on some of the recommendations I heard from this show. There was a great deal of comments made about the relationship of food and nutrition to the intensity of tinnitus. Amongst list of potential culprits, I recognized a few in my life. Caffeine was at the top of the list, and between my coffee and my diet cokes I always had something I was sipping on all day. Between my coffee and my diet coke, I was consuming a lot of caffeine every day. When I quit smoking, I substituted coffee and diet coke as my addiction and bandaid for stress. I was drinking a huge amount of fluids, but very little of it was plain water. Alcohol was another one listed by these doctors as a contributor to the existing problem, and on nights when I couldn't sleep from the noise, I had a few drinks to help me sleep. Vitamin deficiency and especially B12 was also high on the list. Vitamins were something I took on a hit and miss basis. I made the decision to control these three things and see what would happen. I didn't believe I could do it all at once, so I made a schedule where I cut back a little more each day. I made little baggies of my daily vitamins and made sure B12 was among them and I switched to decaf coffee. I didn't want to stop all my caffeine right away, so I after a few days I started to trade some of my diet cokes for soda with a squeeze of orange juice for sweetness and flavor. I cut back my alcohol to having one occasionally and mostly only on weekends with friends over dinner. It took me a few months to change my habits and eliminate the caffeine and some chemicals from my body, but now whether I'm stressed or not I sleep more peacefully with no ringing in my ears. In talking with my friends, I discovered I wasn't the only one with this problem, and when they made changes in their habits, they also saw a difference in their ability to sleep better.

TAKE CONTROL

To get your most restful sleep, start by reviewing your sleeping environment and decide what you can control

1. Your Food. As I discovered what I was consuming interfered with my health and disturbed my sleep. Every body reacts differently to certain foods and beverages. Some foods cause gas or intestinal distress; other food can contribute to congestion. Spicy or fatty foods can cause heartburn. Alcohol may make you sleepy, but it also interferes with the deepest sleep. And going to bed on a full stomach means your digestive system has to stay awake to digest your food. Drinking too

much liquid just before bedtime can cause you to wake up in the middle of the night to go to the bathroom.

2. Your bed. Make sure you have the right bed for your body. Some people sleep more soundly on a firm bed, where others prefer the softer type. Doctors can sometimes prescribe certain types of bed for their patients, especially if they have an underlying medical condition.

3. The light in your room. How much light do you leave on, or let in through windows and open doors. Light interferes with your pineal gland's production of melatonin and serotonin. Melatonin controls your natural cycle of sleeping. Your body naturally produces melatonin; however, light affects how much melatonin your body produces. The less light, the more melatonin should be produced helping to make your sleep more restful.

4. Regulate your sleep cycle with a bedtime routine of going to bed at the same time every night, especially when you get up at the same time every morning.

5. Turn off all sound. Going to sleep with a TV or radio on prevents you from getting your most restful sleep. .While noise machines are useful to drown out the noises from outside, and soft meditation music can lull you into sleep

6. Room temperature. Rooms that are too warm or too cold interfere with your comfort and your sleep.

7. Stop working at least two hours before bedtime. Make your to-do lists for the following day and put all your work away. Do not take it into the bedroom with you. If you stay up late working on that project or presentation that is due tomorrow, do something to clear your mind or you will continue to work on it or worry about it in your sleep. Learn to schedule your work so you can complete projects before the eleventh hour deadline.

8. Stop exercising at least 5 hours before bedtime. Exercise can stimulate your energy and it raises your body temperature. Giving your energy time to return to a more relaxed state will make it easier to sleep. Most healthy people

sleep better when their body is cool and not sweating and overheated (Just ask any menopausal woman). So give your body time to return to it's natural body temperature.

9. Empty your mind. If you have a list of things to do tomorrow in your mind, write them on a list and put the list on your desk or another place where you will find it when you need it in the morning. Keep a pad of paper next to your bed, so if you wake up in the middle of the night with something on your mind that you must remember in the morning, write it down and let it go. This also  applies to anything else that might be bothering you. The more you empty your mind onto the paper, the less you have rummaging around to think about in your sleep.

10. Clear the air. Heavy smells of perfume, food and body odor can interfere with your sleep. Open windows when you can to let the air circulate; use an air purifier (not a scented air spray) to clear the room. Take a shower and keep the sheet of your bed clean and fresh smelling. Using scents that commonly relax, such as lavender sachets or lavender sleep pillows, can be added to a fresh room.

11. Create a going-to-bed ritual. Take a shower or soothing bath, listen to soft music, do a relaxing meditation. After doing these go to bed.

Almost everyone has a sleepless night every one in a while. If yours become too often and these remedies don't work, you should consult with a professional. There are herbs, minerals and sleep aids that might be your answer. Since some sleeping drugs can become addictive, they should only be used as a last resort.

© Jerylyn Draker

You can learn more about Jerylyn Draker in the Authors section at the end of this book.

CONCLUSION

You may not have guessed that there could be so many choices, tools and techniques to assist you with your stress. You now have more tools, but they are of no value until you apply them in your life. The more you practice the more prepared you will be for those everyday and unexpected events and circumstances.

Stress is around us everyday. The more you prepare and practice the tools, the more you will show stress who *is* the boss.

When you choose a tool or technique that you have never tried before, or one that you haven't used for a long time, give yourself a chance to adapt to it. Old habits are going to surface, even as you work to establish new ones. Repetition over a few days or a few times will give you a better assessment if your new choice is working for you.

- ❖ Select your favorite.
- ❖ Select one that seems easiest.
- ❖ Select the one that fits your schedule.
- ❖ Select the one that seems like fun.
- ❖ Start with one; then try another until you have embodied some of the tools so that they are almost first nature in your response to stress.

This book has been designed to provide suggestions in the form of comments, testimonials, expert advice and personal stories from people just like you. It is not intended as medical or psychological advice. The results you may receive from following the suggestions in this book are subjective and unique to you. I cannot guarantee that following any of these recommendations will correct the causes of your stress or definitely eliminate the distress you are feeling. You personally possess that responsibility and control. My intention is to provide a variety of solutions that have worked for others, and may work for you.

"Finish each day and be done with it. You have done what you could. Some blunders and absurdities no doubt crept in, forget them as soon as you can. Tomorrow is a new day, you shall begin it well and serenely..."
~ Ralph Waldo Emerson ~

This is not the end of Stress Out solutions. Additional articles, tools, exercises and products are offered in the free Stress Out Daily Tips e-zine. Some of these additional recommendations include: Biofeedback, Hypnotherapy, managing in pieces, games, Tai Chi, time control, learning to say no, setting boundaries and more. I invite you to visit the Stress Out blog to read additional personal experiences and share your own. What you have to say may just be what someone needs to read at just that moment.

There are events and circumstances in life that can be overwhelming. When even the most dedicated efforts to use these and other tools is more than you can handle on your own, support with a coach or counselor may be the solution.

I wish for you a joy filled and healthy life.

GRATITUDE

Because this book involved countless hours of research and even more hours in writing and editing in order to bring together as many helpful stories and advice as possible, I have many people to be grateful for.

First, my deepest gratitude for Spirit for guiding me to research and publish this book which was an answer to several questions I had asked. I am grateful for this spiritual guidance which connected me to everyone who contributed to making this book a reality; for guiding me when I felt lost and shining a light on answers when I needed help.

I am thankful for each person that shared their stories with me during my research, and those who gave me permission to print their testimonials - Marcia Bearn, Julie Cucina, Tracy Gelfer, Michelle Granger, Cameron Grover, Precilla Junart, Barbara Kramer, Lisa Lorie, Tracy Marine, Pat Mynor, Cathi Polenetic, Brad Smorther and Marcie Taylor. I appreciate each co-author for their wisdom and for sharing their expertise and experiences so others can learn from them - Aila Accad, Debra Costanzo, Gina Cotroneo, Jerilynn Draker, Beverly Edelstein, Monika Klein, Nancy Miiller, Veronica Ray, Ellen Whitehurst and Melissa Whuel. I am grateful for all the wise words that are quoted and placed strategically in the book to support the message of the chapter.

I feel special gratitude for each person who inspires me and supports me on my journey. Allorah Meilani for helping me to remember my strength and purpose on a particularly difficult day. Ellen DeGeneres for many hours of healing laughter and stress-free dancing. Sarah Ferguson, Oprah and Louise Hay for being such exquisite role models and proponents of possibilities. Rev. Dr. Michael Beckwith, Marianne Williamson and Thich Nhat Hahn for being my spiritual guides. Zig Ziglar, Gary & Maggie Rosales, Michelle Hazelwood and Lorraine Jackson for being examples of living in Faith. Dr. Mehmet Oz for health answers that addressed some of my personal concerns, as well as those of many other women I met. Walter Davis for caring and patience. My loving friends who remind me that "I'm worth it." Special gratitude to my Angel, Marge Diehl for being my cheerleader and for helping to make sure my words made sense.

And thank you to the readers of this book for making the effort to find solutions to your stress. The changes we make in each of our lives create ripple effects which add to the changes in the world for all of us to enjoy.

CONTRIBUTING AUTHORS

SUMNER M. DAVENPORT
Author, Publisher

Sumner Davenport's deepest passion is seeing people empowering others while living the life of their dreams. She encourages others to question their premature cognitive commitments and discover their own answers for their lives.

A real life example of an impassioned visionary, Sumner began her career at age nine when she opened her first lemonade stand and a backyard carnival. Throughout her childhood she was inspired by the successful business people she saw. She used this early education as a foundation when she started her first of many unique and interesting entrepreneurial ventures at age 19.

Although Sumner is the recipient of several awards and acknowledgements, she credits her best education to *The University of Hard Knocks*, with crash courses in *taking risks* and advanced learning from *bouncing back*. For several years Sumner has advocated for Self Investment rather than self-improvement. Throughout the twists, turns and painful bumps in her life, she has rebuilt her self-esteem by reminding herself that who she is, is not based on who other people judge her to be, nor their acceptance of her.

People are attracted to Sumner for her positive resilience and her willingness to share the secrets to her own success. She has been deemed the **"Bounce-Back Expert"** with a mystical quality. She is sought after as a speaker on several topics. Based on experience, research and proven techniques Sumner delivers customized presentations with appropriate humor and energy. She is described as "streetwise", charismatic and sincere. She amuses, educates, inspires, delights and motivates in each customized presentation which also include personal stories of her own "failures" and successes.

Sumner believes that in order for positive change to occur in destructive situations, individuals must be willing to speak up and take action. A passion for the future of today's youth, and a belief that our future is in their hands, Sumner works with select charitable organizations that assist young people with their life options. She has received acknowledgement from the Child Advocates office of the Los Angeles Superior Court, for her "Outstanding Service to Children", as a Court Appointed Special Advocate (CASA) Guardian ad Litem.

She has co-authored several books and she is quoted often. One of Sumner's quotes was voted to be included in the Top 10 Healthy Thoughts of 2007.

She can be reached through her website:
www.sumnerdavenport.com
or email: sumner@sumnerdavenport.com

AILA ACCAD, RN, MSN
Aila Accad, "Your Stress-Busters Coach" is an award-winning speaker, best-selling author and certified well-being coach for 40 years, who specializes in quick ways to release stress and reclaim that energy to live your fullest life and achieve your highest purpose.

After teaching stress-management for over 25 years, Aila had a stress crisis, which led to an instant stress breakthrough. She just published her findings in the new Amazon best-seller, "34 Instant Stress-Busters, Quick tips to de-stress fast with no extra time or money."

As president & founder of LifeQuest International, LLC, she is an innovator in business training and coaching. Aila creates unique, simple, down to earth experiences to help audiences and clients easily connect to themselves and the message. Thousands of people have reclaimed freedom in their lives through the application of her groundbreaking process, "Breaking the Perfection Myth". She is an innovator who is able to break down barriers for expanded thinking, creativity and relationship building. Her audiences are transformed and delighted.

Aila holds bachelors and master's degrees in nursing with continuing course work in family systems therapy, addiction recovery, women's issues, business, personal growth and employee assistance consulting, and is additionally credentialed as a Certified Comprehensive Coach, Reiki Master and Emotional Freedom Techniques Advanced Practitioner.

She is past president and current vice-president of the West Virginia Nurses Association, past board member of the Charleston Area Chamber of Commerce, recipient of Business Woman of the Year Award and designated Distinguished Toastmaster by Toastmasters International. Her biography appears in Who's Who in American Nursing and Who's Who of Women Executives.

Aila's best-sellers include "34 Instant Stress-Busters, Quick tips to de-stress fast with no extra time or money", Flowing Owl Press, 2009 and "Living in the Now", part of the best selling Wake-Up Live the Life You Love series, Little Seed Press, 2009. Her books and programs are available at http://www.ailaspeaks.com.

DEBRA COSTANZO

Debra Costanzo is Founder and CEO of "3 in 1 Fitness" by D. L. Costanzo, LLC. Debra has been interested in health and fitness since her early teens. However, after working in the corporate world for over 30 years and experiencing a high level of stress first-hand, she realized the importance of taking personal responsibility for her own health and wellness. This realization placed a burning desire in her heart to coach those types of individuals with whom she could most personally relate: Corporate Executives, Senior Management, and other busy professionals.

Busy professionals are over-tired, over-stressed, over-worked and, sometimes, overweight. They have sacrificed their health for their wealth. While executives are trying to make a million bucks, Debra is helping them look like a million bucks! It's her goal to help business leaders establish better lifestyle choices so they can reduce their stress, as well as their waistlines. Healthy living doesn't have to be painful. It doesn't have to be difficult. It is her desire to be a partner to her clients...someone with whom they can co-create, achieve, and experience goal realization. She desires to be their confidante` with whom they can feel safe enough to share, express, and admit set-backs and/or roadblocks --- as well as celebrate victories. It can be fun and energizing as Debra paves the way, helping her clients to set realistic and attainable fitness goals. Debra believes her clients will always be in a state of moving forward, regardless of where the client is in the process. "Failure" will not be a result, a definition of condition, or a definition for a lack of progress. She believes she and her clients are on a dynamic wellness journey towards success.

Debra birthed the name of her coaching practice to depict her goal coaching leaders to be "fit" in body, mind, and spirit. Debra aims to improve the overall health of business leaders, one life at a time. Debra can be reached through her website www.3in1fitness.com, or email debracostanzo@3in1fitness.com

GINA COTRONEO

Soul's Calling was founded by President Gina Cotroneo in Dallas in 2004. The company creates and markets a "fashion-with-a-purpose" accessory and gift line.

Soul's Calling's credo is to advertise positive ideas and energy. Ms. Cotroneo knows firsthand the creative power that we hold inside ourselves. She believes that all experiences are gifts, to realize this is to evolve, and to live this is to have true power. That philosophy was proven in a most unlikely way after a violent attack in 1997. She chose to see the event as an opportunity, and turned the experience into positive action.

Her story of courage and self-empowerment has been featured on television programs such as "Oprah," "Montel," and "Crier Live" and in such publications as Glamour. Oprah Winfrey said of Ms. Cotroneo, "She tapped into the kind of power that can never be taken away."

"We are all connected with one another, and our individual actions and words have a great effect on the whole," said Cotroneo. Positive Energy Transfer (PET) is a very important component to the Soul's Calling brand. "I send conscious positive energy into all the products by means of prayer and meditation, with the intent that they carry joy wherever they go. Requests for awareness and conscious creation are also made to the manufacturers as a way of helping to ensure that each product contains the highest "vibe" possible in addition to its more obvious positive message." The positive energy is held in the product and transferred to the user and from that person to another. And another. And so the consciousness of the world is raised and it becomes a better place.

Designer Gina Cotroneo is also a motivational speaker. She has received numerous awards for her leadership and community contributions. " She can be reached through her website www.soulscalling.com or email gina@soulscalling.com

JERYLYN DRAKER

As an avid movie buff, Jerylyn was always standing in line at the theaters, but she became frustrated when the movie choices seemed limited to violence, hatred and social demise. Frustrated she looked for alternatives, and found Movies with Message. As an associate, she enjoys sharing reviews and recommendations for movies that uplift and inspire. Jerylyn is very involved as a volunteer in local children's organizations and hospitals, lending support to those in need. She has also participated several years in a row for Team in Training to raise funds for leukemia. Jerylyn can be reached through: www.MovieswithMessage.com or email: info@movieswithmessage.com

BEVERLY EDELSTEIN

Beverly Edelstein is an advertising executive with a California magazine publication. For over 15 years she has educated her clients about the importance of targeted print advertising. "Effective advertising is a science; and advertising let's people know you are still in business."

Believing that community service and volunteering is a very important part of our being; Beverly has been trained and certified to operate a crisis hot line for victims of abuse who are seeking information and support. "Sometimes a person just needs to vent, and speaking to a stranger is their safest way of communicating their crisis. Knowing what to say without pushing them over the edge can save a life. Getting them to understand the importance of coming to a shelter for safety, can be the difference between life and death." She also volunteers at a local shelter in Southern California, giving support and educating abused women and children about the signs of abuse and reminding them that there is a better lifestyle possible for them. Beverly conducts classes and leads discussion groups on ways to restart their life, which include using vision boards to display their goals.

 **MONIKA KLEIN, BS, CN**

Clinical Nutritionist, Teacher, and Health and Wellness Spokesperson Monika Klein has many years in clinical practice offering her own unique health counseling skills and experience. She counsels in the areas of diet and nutrition, lifestyle, healthy exercise, supplementation and stress management. Through hormone balancing, weight loss and detoxification programs; clients see remarkable results in their overall health.

After graduating from the University of Manitoba in Canada she began actively working in broadcast journalism and television production for several years. She then returned to private practice and established a very successful health practice in the Los Angeles area. With private clients, national and international lectures at leading health conferences, as a published writer, as a college professor and finally in her own local cable show entitled Total Health Talk, Monika continues to spread her message of health.

Monika's compassionate and caring approach to healing is certainly refreshing. You will feel heard and cared about, with a sense of hope and inspiration. To help you devise a health program she draws on her educational background, clinical experience and highly developed intuition. Monika believes that true health comes from the body's ability to heal itself. She therefore, has developed profoundly beneficial programs which will help you to become more and more empowered in your health and in your life.

While becoming healthier you will also become increasingly educated about how your body works and what it needs to stay healthy, fit and whole. Monica Klein can be reached through her website www.coachingforhealth.com or email: monika@coachingforhealth.com

NANCY MIILLER

Nancy Miiller is a spiritual coach, course & workshop facilitator, ordained ministerial counselor, Flower Essence practitioner, energy healer, article writer, ceremonial writer, and co-founder of Reconnect from Within®. She believes that we are all students and teachers to each other, and that life is a learning experience originating from the inside out; hence, Reconnect from Within®.

Nancy started her professional career 20+ years ago, as a graphic designer following her love of art and photography. After many years in the design industry, she successfully completed her MBA in Marketing in 2004 at Western International University in Phoenix, Arizona. In completing her degree, Nancy utilized her thesis in examining the topic of 'Spirituality in Business' thus giving her the knowledge and confidence to launch Reconnect from Within® a few years later.

Nancy's spiritual journey truly awakened around the year 2000. At the time she filled herself with all kinds of self-help and spiritual books, all gifts in guiding her inward to Higher Self/Spirit. During this process she became interested in energy healing and all things metaphysical. She studied all levels of QuantumPathic® energy healing, Reconnective Healing® and The Reconnection® with Dr. Eric Pearl D.C., and Egyptian Healing Rods. She continued to expand her learning of energy healing by studying Flower Essences and graduated from the course at Australasian College.

A turning point happened for Nancy, as she became a student of *A Course in Miracles* and *Disappearance of the Universe*. "It felt only of Truth, beyond anything else I have read or experienced. True healing and forgiveness began and a new perspective on life shined through."

With this philosophy in place, in 2007, Nancy and her business partner PJ Bouchard formed, Reconnect from Within®. In a safe and nurturing environment, Nancy coaches and facilitates others in awakening to their Higher Self/Spirit for inner peace and love, along with inspired knowledge and guidance to apply to their daily life.

In 2008, Nancy became an Ordained Ministerial Counselor with Pathways of Light Spiritual College of Kiel, Wisconsin. Through the mini4sterial program, Nancy has been certified as an Accessing Inner Wisdom Counselor and is also certified to facilitate Pathways of Light Courses and workshops.

Nancy also loves to write ceremonies for any and all events that anyone can do at home by themselves, or with family or friends. She also loves yoga, gardening, photography, Italian wines, cooking, and to share all these things with her significant other Paul.

Nancy can be reached through her website: www.reconnectfromwithin.com or email, nmiiller@reconnectfromwithin.com Loving to connect with you.

VERONICA "RONI" RAY

Roni is an associate with a company that helps people to remember the power of gratitude. To Roni, Thank and Grow Richer means that our lives continue to be enriched as we appreciate people, events and definitely ourselves.

Since the advent of the computer, email has taken the place of communication, and saying thank you has been reduced to an occasional "thanks". For over 2 years, Roni has worked with a greeting card business/service company titled: Thank and Grow Richer. Her services help businesses to remember their clients on special days, thank them for referrals and keep in touch on a regular basis. Busy people use her services to remember their friends on special dates such as birthdays, anniversaries and promotions.

Her website offers this personalized card mailing service, as well as and links to many free e-cards and other gifts so busy people can always remember to say Thank You.

You can reach Roni thought the website: www.ThanksandGrowRicher.com or by email: info@thankandgrowricher.com

ELLEN WHITEHURST

Ellen Whitehurst is a world renowned and recognized Feng Shui author and expert. She writes a monthly marquee column for Redbook magazine that blends her expertise in astrology with that of Feng Shui (appropriately called 'Shuistrology'), as well as pen 'The Feng Shui Tip of the Day' for iVillage.com. Her first book, "Make This Your Lucky Day: Feng Shui Secrets, etc" was published and released by Random House in 2008. She is, as well, a regular contributor and considered Feng Shui expert for 'Natural Health' and 'Woman's World' magazines as well as on line expert for 'RealSavvyMom.com' and 'FreshStartAfterDivorce.com'. She regularly and monthly guests on six syndicated radio shows such as Good Morning America's 'It's A New Day with Richard and Lori' and 'The Bob and Sheri Show' both nationally syndicated with a listening audience in more than 1000 markets.

She currently has a best selling line of bookmarks (Feng Shui Flat pen Bookmarks by Ellen Whitehurst) and is in process of discussing two new product offerings. And, although she has partnered and contributed to many manufactured product promotions and collaborations in the past, including the super success that her 'Feng Shui In A Cup' promotion had with Starbucks. Inside an intended 14 week promotion, every 'Feng Shui In A Cup' piece sold out in a record 5 ½ weeks. As well, the first and only time that in house baristas were taking names on a "waiting list" in the case more cups hit their shelves. 75,000 units of 'Feng Shui In A Cup' sold in a record 5 ½ weeks off Starbucks store shelves, the first and to date ONLY successful sell through of any sideline item that they have ever "experienced." Ellen's line of Feng Shui jewelry is an extension of a product process that promises to empower and to enhance. Feng Shui jewelry holds the promise and the power to activate fortune and luck for whoever wears it. Ellen Whitehurst wishes us all great fortunes and GOOD LUCK!

Ellen can be reached through her website:
www.ellenwhitehurst.com

MELISSA WHUEL

Melissa Whuel works as an assistant to a financial analyst. She appreciates being able to work with an employer who helps people understand the results of their money decisions, and educates them on their possibilities. As a single mom of two boys, she enjoys being involved in their many activities, including all their sports which help to keep her young.

SELF INVESTMENT PUBLISHING
is a publisher and a retailer of self help books.

We also offer design, editing, marketing and publishing services to new authors, as well as joint venture and co author opportunities.

PLUS we offer a unique niche marketing program designed reach your target market and separate you from the competition. It's not about books, it's really about reaching your target market!

www.SelfInvestmentPublishing.com

PRODUCTS & RESOURCES

Mindful Video mentioned in Mindfulness chapter
Visit this website:
http://viscog.beckman.illinois.edu/flashmovie/15.php

Your assignment, should you decide to accept it, is to COUNT the number of basketball "passes" made by the WHITE SHIRTED TEAM ONLY. The video will move fast so keep your eyes on the white shirts. The correct answer is at the end of this section.

Recent Studies say that we need at least 12 laughs a day to stay healthy.

Visit www.stressout-book.com/stress-resources.htm
to watch this short free video.

Mindful Video answer:

In your mindfulness test, did you see the gorilla in the room? You didn't?
Sorry, the test was really not about counting passes between the white shirts. It was to see if you were aware of what will be obvious to you the next time you run that video. The gorilla even beat his chest to try and get your attention. Now slide the little button back to the left on that video and watch it again. If you still didn't see him, check your pulse.
By the way, there were 14 passes.
If you didn't see the gorilla on the first viewing, you're in good company. So many people go through life only seeing portions of what is available to them. Now that you are aware of the gorilla, did you go back and watch the movie again? Did you see the gorilla? If you did, it was because you were mindfully looking at the video this time, expecting to see the gorilla.

YOU MAKE THE DIFFERENCE

All things are possible...

The Foundation's primary mission is to provide scholarships for secondary education for children who have lost a parent to breast cancer.

www.PearlsofHope.com

Pearls of Hope® is a registered trademark of The Lorraine Jackson Foundation, a California 501(c)(3) non-profit organization.

CASA
Court Appointed Special Advocates

GIVE A CHILD A VOICE

In the United States over one half million children are in foster care because they cannot safely live with their families. Nearly 70,000 National CASA volunteers serve approximately 280,000 of those abused or neglected children every year.

www.casaforchildren.org

Quote References:

The following are the originators of some of the quotes, people and sources that have inspired me throughout the years which are included in this book.

Marcus Aurelius Antoninus Augustus (121 – 180) Roman emperor from 161 to his death in 180. He was the last of the "Five Good Emperors", and is also considered one of the most important Stoic philosophers.

Louisa May Alcott (1832 –1888) American novelist, best known for the novel *Little Women.*

Aesop, from the Greek (620-560 BC), known only for the genre of fables ascribed to him, was by tradition a slave who was a contemporary of Croesus and Peisistratus in the mid-sixth century BC in ancient Greece.

Bhagavad Gita (Song of God) is one of the most important Hindu scriptures. It is revered as a sacred scripture of Hinduism, and considered as one of the most important philosophical classics of the world.

L. Frank Baum, author of The Wonderful Wizard of Oz, and thirteen other novels based on the land of Oz.

Henry Ward Beecher (1813-1887) Liberal US Congregational minister

The Bible, King James Version is an English translation of the Christian Bible completed in 1611 by the Church of England.

Erma Bombeck (1927-1996) U.S. humorist and author of several books.

Warren Edward Buffett is a U.S. investor, businessman, and philanthropist. He is one of the most successful investors in history.

George F. Burns (1896 –1996), born Nathan Birnbaum, was an American comedian, actor, and writer.

Joseph Campbell (1904 – 1987) was an American mythologist, writer and lecturer, best known for his work in comparative mythology and comparative religion.

Alan Cohen, M.A. is the author of 22 popular inspirational books and CD's, including the best-selling *The Dragon Doesn't Live Here Anymore*, the award-winning *A Deep Breath of Life*, and the classic *Are You as Happy as Your Dog?*

Robert Collier (1885-1950 Author and progressive publisher who strongly believed that happiness and abundance were within easy reach.

William Henry "Bill" Cosby, Jr. is an American comedian, actor, author, television producer, musician and activist.

Wayne Walter Dyer is an American self-help advocate, author and lecturer.

Albert Einstein (1879 – 1955) was a theoretical physicist best known for his theories of special relativity and general relativity. He is often regarded as the father of modern physics.

Epictetus (Greek: c.55–c.135) A Greek Stoic philosopher.

Clarissa Pinkola Estés, Ph.D. is an American poet, psychoanalyst and post-trauma specialist. She is a certified Jungian psychoanalyst who has practiced clinically for 38 years. She has also been a post-trauma specialist at Columbine High School in Littleton, Colorado. She is the author of many books on the life of the soul, and her book, *Women Who Run With the Wolves* was on the New York Times Best Seller list for 145 weeks.

Harvey S. Firestone, (1868-1938) American industrialist founder of the Firestone Tire & Rubber Co.,

Harry Emerson Fosdick (1878- 1969) American clergyman.

Epictetus (AD 55–AD 135) was a Greek Stoic philosopher.

Charles Haanel (1866 - 1949)was a noted American New Thought author and a businessman best known for his contributions to the New Thought Movement through his book The Master Key System.

Shakti Gawain is an author and proponent of what she calls "personal development".

Oliver Wendell Holmes (1809-1894), American Physician, Harvard Professor, Poet, Writer, and Humorist

Aldous Huxley (1894 – 1963) was an English writer best known for his novels including Brave New World.

William James (1842 –1910) A pioneering American psychologist and philosopher trained as a medical doctor. He wrote influential books on the young science of psychology, educational psychology, psychology of religious experience and mysticism, and the philosophy of pragmatism.

Steven "Steve" Jobs is an American businessman, and the co-founder of Apple Inc.

Kabbalah is a discipline and school of thought concerned with the mystical aspect of Judaism.

Henry Alfred Wolfgang Kissinger pronounced is a German-born American political scientist, diplomat, and winner of the Nobel Peace Prize. He served as National Security Advisor and later concurrently as Secretary of State in the Nixon Administration.

Jiddu Krishnamurti (1895–1986) was a renowned writer and speaker on philosophical and spiritual subjects. He constantly stressed the need for a revolution in the psyche of every human being and emphasized that such revolution cannot be brought about by any external entity, be it religious, political, or social.

C. W. Leadbeater (1854 - 1934) was an English clergyman, author, clairvoyant, and prominent early member of the Theosophical Society.

Nicephorus the Solitary, Thirteenth century Christian monk at Constantinople and then on Mount Athos.

Friedrich Nietzsche (1844 – 1900)German philosopher of the late 19th century who challenged the foundations of Christianity and traditional morality.

Sylvia Plath (1932 –1963) American poet, novelist, children's author, and short story author.

Publius Ovidius Naso (43 BC – AD 18), known as **Ovid** in the English-speaking world, was a Roman poet who wrote about love, seduction, and mythological transformation.

Camille Pissarro (1830 – 1903) was a French Impressionist painter.

Theodore Roosevelt (1858 – 1919) was the 26th President of the United States

Francoise Sagan (1935 – 2004)was a French playwright, novelist, and screenwriter.

Sanskrit, one of the liturgical languages of Hinduism and Buddhism,

Albert Schweitzer (1875 - 1965) was an Alsatian German-French theologian, musician, philosopher, and physician.

Hans Hugo Bruno Selye, (1907-1982) was a Canadian endocrinologist of Austro-Hungarian origin and Hungarian ethnicity. Selye did much important factual work on the hypothetical non-specific response of the organism to stressors

Lucius Annaeus Seneca (c. 4 BC – AD 65) was a Roman Stoic philosopher, statesman, dramatist, and in one work humorist, of the Silver Age of Latin literature. He was tutor and later advisor to emperor Nero.

Serenity prayer, A prayer that has been adopted by several twelve-step programs and spiritual self-help groups.

Shankaracharya, is a commonly used title of heads of monasteries in the Advaita tradition.

Brenda Stuart, author and life coach living in New Mexico.

Mother Teresa (1910 – 1997) Mother Teresa was an Albanian Roman Catholic nun who founded the Missionaries of Charity and won the Nobel Peace Prize in 1979 for her humanitarian work.

Lao-tzu, Tao te Ching, is a Chinese classic text which praises self-gained knowledge with emphasis on that knowledge being gained with humility

Denis E. Waitley (1933 - present), is an American motivational speaker and writer, consultant and best-selling author.

Woodrow Wilson (1856–1924)[1] was the 28th President of the United States.

John Wayne (Marion Mitchell Morrison) (1907 –1979) was a larger than life, American film actor, director and producer.

Walter Winchell was an American newspaper and radio commentator.

The Upanishads are Hindu scriptures that constitute the core teachings of Vedanta.

Made in the USA
Charleston, SC
16 December 2009